Twayne's English Authors Series

Sylvia E. Bowman, *Editor*

INDIANA UNIVERSITY

Christina Rossetti

TEAS 201

Christina Rossetti and her mother,
portrait by Dante Gabriel Rossetti

CHRISTINA ROSSETTI

By RALPH A. BELLAS

Illinois State University

TWAYNE PUBLISHERS

A DIVISION OF G. K. HALL & CO., BOSTON

Library of Congress Cataloging in Publication Data

Bellas, Ralph A
  Christina Rossetti.

  (Twayne's English authors series ; TEAS 201)
  Bibliography: p. 127–34.
  Includes index.
  1. Rossetti, Christina Georgina, 1830 - 1894.
  2. Authors, English — 19th century — Biography.
  PR5238.B44   1977   821'.8 [B]   76-29711
  ISBN 0-8057-6671-5

To

Louise

and

Christine, Ralph, Marcia,
Gregory, Kimberly, Laurence

Contents

About the Author

Ralph A. Bellas received his undergraduate degree from The Catholic University of America, his M.A. from the University of Pennsylvania, and his Ph.D. from the University of Kansas. His dissertation on William Morris stimulated his interest in the Pre-Raphaelites; the present volume, *Christina Rossetti*, is a product of that interest. His publications include articles on composition and critical book reviews on Victorian authors. He has taught at the University of Kansas and Villanova University; he now teaches at Illinois State University.

Preface

Many twentieth-century literary historians have been uncertain about the place of Christina Rossetti among the Victorian poets; but in recent years her position has stabilized. In many respects, she is now seen as a representative figure of the period; indeed, she is regarded as one of its distinguished poets but falls short perhaps of being ranked among the foremost Victorians. In her own day, she first gained recognition with the publication of *Goblin Market and Other Poems* in 1862. Subsequent volumes added to her reputation, mainly in her late years as a writer of religious verse. Following her death in 1894, an outpouring of tributes in obituary notices, memorials, and reminiscences attested to her high standing among contemporaries. But, shortly after the turn of the century, her literary position declined.

The centenary of her birth in 1930 brought a revival of interest that lasted for several years and resulted in the publication of a number of books and articles. By 1935, critical attention subsided; and she seemed all but forgotten for the next twenty-five years. Since even anthologists either ignored her completely or minimized their selections, most readers who knew anything of her work became acquainted with it by way of a few poems such as "Goblin Market," "When I am Dead, My Dearest," "Oh Roses for the Flush of Youth," and one or two pieces from *Sing-Song*, her collection of children's poetry. But interest has again revived; and, since 1959, several fairly extensive selected editions of her poetry have been published; period and Pre-Raphaelite anthologies now include a generous number of her poems that indicate the range of her achievement; and critical reevaluations in general acknowledge her significance in the literary history of the second half of the nineteenth century.

Until recently much of the criticism about Christina Rossetti tended to be more concerned with her life than with a close examination of her poetry. In this study, biographical information is used, but no attempt is made to develop a detailed chronology of events. Emphasis falls on her poetry, but attention is also given to her prose. Nevertheless, because Christina is a very personal writer, the study reveals much of her inner life as reflected in her works. As a poet she matured rapidly. Some of her best poems came early in life. Many of them, written at various ages, illustrate similar techniques and repeat similar moods and themes. Chapters 1 and 2 cover Christina's background and early poetry. The following two chapters examine her major secular or general poems as separate from the devotional and religious ones, though a sharp distinction cannot always be maintained. Chapter 5 offers an analysis of her two sonnet sequences. Chapter 6 considers her devotional poems. Succeeding chapters discuss her children's verse, short stories, and religious prose. Chapter 10 concludes the study with an evaluation of her literary achievement.

I am grateful to the late George R. Canning, Jr., to Robert L. Duncan, Stanley W. Renner, and Robert D. Sutherland for many suggestions while this book was in manuscript. I also want to thank members of the staff of Milner Library, Illinois State University, for their assistance. Finally, I wish to express my appreciation to Mrs. Jack C. Carr for her interest and help.

RALPH A. BELLAS

Illinois State University

Chronology

1830   Christina Georgina Rossetti born December 5 in London, last of four children of Gabriele Rossetti and Frances Polidori Rossetti.

1847   *Verses*. First volume of poems. Privately printed by her grandfather, Gaetano Polidori.

1848   Pre-Raphaelite Brotherhood formed in September. Though not a formal member, Christina has a close association with the Brotherhood. Declines a proposal of marriage from James Collinson, a painter and member of the Brotherhood, and then later accepts, but in 1850 cancels the engagement. Comes before the public with a poem in the October 14 issue of *The Athenaeum*, followed by another on October 21.

1850   Contributes seven lyrics to *The Germ*, the Pre-Raphaelite journal.

1851–   Helps mother in day school at Mornington Crescent, and at
1852   Frome, Sommerset, in 1853.

1854   Death of father.

1861   First trip abroad with her mother and brother, William Michael.

1862   *Goblin Market and Other Poems*.

1865   Second trip abroad with her mother and William Michael.

1866   *The Prince's Progress and Other Poems*. Declines a proposal of marriage from Charles Bagot Cayley, a close family friend and man of letters, probably because of his unorthodox religious views.

1870   *Commonplace and Other Short Stories*.

1871   Contracts Graves' disease.

1872   *Sing-Song: A Nursery Rhyme Book*.

1873   Maria Francesca Rossetti, her sister, joins the All Saints' Sisterhood.

1874   *Annus Domini: A Prayer for Each Day of the Year, Founded on a Text of Holy Scripture. Speaking Likenesses.*

1875   *Goblin Market, The Prince's Progress, and Other Poems.* First collected edition.

1876   Death of Maria Francesca Rossetti.

1879   *Seek and Find: A Double Series of Short Studies of the Benedicite.*

1881   *A Pageant and Other Poems. Called to be Saints: the Minor Festivals Devotionally Studied.*

1882   Death of her brother, Dante Gabriel Rossetti.

1883   *Letter and Spirit: Notes on the Commandments.*

1885   *Time Flies: A Reading Diary.*

1886   Death of mother.

1890   *Poems: New and Enlarged Edition.* Second collected edition.

1892   Christina suffering from cancer. *The Face of the Deep: A Devotional Commentary on the Apocalypse.*

1893   *Verses.* A collection of poems reprinted from *Called to be Saints, Time Flies,* and *The Face of the Deep.*

1894   Christina dies on December 29.

1896   *New Poems, Hitherto Unpublished or Uncollected,* ed. William Michael Rossetti.

1897   *Maude: A Story for Girls.*

1904   *The Poetical Works of Christina Georgina Rossetti, with Memoir and Notes,* ed. William Michael Rossetti.

CHAPTER 1

Background

I *Family*

WHEN Christina Rossetti's father, Gabriele Rossetti, came to England in 1824, he was a political exile from Italy. In his native land he had been a popular poet, especially adept at improvisation, a librettist, and a curator of statuary at the Royal Museum in Naples. Having become involved, somewhat naively but zealously, in the fluctuating political life of the kingdom of Naples, he was forced eventually to flee first to Malta and then to London. He became a tutor of Italian; and, in 1826 he married Frances Polidori, whose father Gaetano Polidori was also an Italian and a well-known poet, translator, and lexicographer. The marriage was a happy one, though Gabriele was seventeen years older than his wife. Their four children were born in successive years: Maria Francesca in 1827, Dante Gabriel (christened Gabriel Charles Dante) in 1828, William Michael in 1829, and Christina Georgina on December 5, 1830. In 1831, Gabriele was appointed Professor of Italian at King's College, a position he held until 1847 when ill health and approaching blindness forced him to resign. He lingered in suffering and often in despair until his death in 1854.

Although the home life of the Rossettis was austere in some respects, it was nevertheless artistically stimulating; and all of the children were destined to make their mark in the world of letters. Maria became well known for her commentary on *The Divine Comedy*; Dante Gabriel became England's foremost Pre-Raphaelite painter and poet; William Michael became a noted critic, essayist, translator, biographer, and editor; Christina, with the publication of *Goblin Market and Other Poems* in 1862, became one of the leading poets of her day. Though the youngest of the children, she was first to achieve public recognition as a writer.

Frances Rossetti was such a pillar of the family that her husband and her children readily acknowledged her as their "guiding light." At her death, William Michael said that she was "the pattern to me of everything that is simple, sweet, kind, and noble."[1] Although his statement well expressed the sentiment of the others, Christina of all the children particularly developed a deep and abiding relationship with her mother over a period of almost fifty-six years during which they were rarely separated for more than a few weeks. Christina often referred to her as a saint, and she dedicated almost all of her books to her. In 1881, for the dedication of *A Pageant and Other Poems*, she addressed a sonnet to her; and, when William Michael published *The Poetical Works of Christina Georgina Rossetti* in 1904, he thought this sonnet the most appropriate final dedication for Christina's collected poems. It is a tribute of Christina's great love for her mother:

> Sonnets are full of love, and this my tome
> Has many sonnets: so here now shall be
> One sonnet more, a love sonnet, from me
> To her whose heart is my heart's quiet home,
> To my first Love, my Mother, on whose knee
> I learnt love-lore that is not troublesome;
> Whose service is my special dignity,
> And she my lodestar while I go and come.
> And so because you love me, and because
> I love you, Mother, I have woven a wreath
> Of rhymes wherewith to crown your honoured name:
> In you not fourscore years can dim the flame
> Of love, whose blessed glow transcends the laws
> Of time and change and mortal life and death.
>
> (lxxiii)[2]

English in temperament and matriarchal in bearing, Mrs. Rossetti was intelligent and immensely self-controlled. "I always had a passion for intellect," she said at seventy; "and my wish was that my husband should be distinguished for intellect, and my children too. I have had my wish; and I now wish that there were a little less intellect in the family, so as to allow for a little more common sense."[3] In desiring more common sense in the family, she was probably thinking not only of her husband, who had spent much of his life searching for esoteric meaning in Dante and issuing antipapal polemics, but also of Dante Gabriel, who had early lived apart from the family in a sometimes shocking Bohemian fashion.

II *Education*

In middle-class Victorian families that could not afford to hire a governess, the mother usually assumed the responsibility for educating the children; and such was the case in the Rossetti household. A governess herself before marriage, Mrs. Rossetti undertook the education of Maria and Christina with the intention of their also becoming governesses. Maria's first position was with the Reverend Lord Charles Thynne in 1844; and, when she left that post, Christina succeeded her for a brief period. Afterward, Christina tutored at home and elsewhere; but, because of frequent illnesses, she could not work regularly. She was, moreover, constitutionally not well suited for teaching. Nevertheless, in 1851–52 at Mornington Crescent, London, and again in 1853 at Frome, Somerset, she assisted Mrs. Rossetti in conducting day schools; but their enterprise proved unsuccessful.

Dante Gabriel and William Michael likewise received their early education from their mother. Then, after a brief stay at a private school, they enrolled in 1837 in King's College School, where their father held his professorship. From 1841 to 1845, Dante Gabriel attended an art academy in Bloomsbury. In late 1845, he was admitted to the Antique School of the Royal Academy. After two years he left, and, for a short time in 1848, he studied under the painter Ford Madox Brown before striking out on his own. In 1845, William became a clerk at the Inland Revenue Board, a position he held until 1894.

The children's education under Mrs. Rossetti dealt chiefly with instruction in languages (English, French, Italian), literature, and religion. In Italian, the children became quite proficient; and Christina later composed some Italian poems. Mrs. Rossetti, a good storyteller, regularly read to the children while they were young, but the literature was rather restricted. Other than the Bible, the usual fare consisted of such works as John Bunyan's *Pilgrim's Progress*, which Christina liked, and novels with a strong moral bias, which she did not at first like.

III *Religion*

Most of the reading was closely related to the children's religious instruction, with which Mrs. Rossetti showed most concern. In early life an Evangelical in the Church of England, she came under the influence of the Oxford reformers, Edward Pusey, John Keble, Hurrell Froude, John Henry Newman, and their followers; and she became a devout Anglo-Catholic in the Church. She was literal and un-questioning in her beliefs. Maria, who was much the same, eventual-ly joined in 1873 the Anglican All Saints' Sisterhood. On that occa-sion Dante Gabriel wrote to his mother: "She will indeed be a great loss, being much the healthiest in mind and cheeriest of us all, ex-cept yourself. William comes next, and Christina and I are nowhere."[4] Though sharing the strong religious disposition of her mother and sister, Christina did not share the same degree of cer-tainty that marked their faith. All four children were baptized in the Church of England, and all four attended church with Mrs. Rossetti. When the two boys reached their early teens, however, they discon-tinued churchgoing.

The spiritual drama enacted in the Rossetti family must have been similar to that taking place in other Victorian families, and it might even be said to typify the religious agitations of the Victorian Age. The mother, with an Evangelical background, is intrigued by the Oxford Movement and becomes a staunch Anglo-Catholic. Under her influence, the two daughters who follow in her footsteps have different reactions: the older Maria has strong convictions; the younger Christina, less firm convictions and religious stability. The father, once a Roman Catholic, becomes antipapal and antiprelatical and, though still a nominal Catholic, is a Freemason. One son, Wil-liam, at fourteen declares himself an agnostic, remains a freethinker throughout his life, and espouses leftist social and political views. The other son, Dante Gabriel, professes no formal religion, sub-scribes at times to theism, but is essentially a nonbeliever.

The Rossetti family lived in a veritable religious maelstrom. The situation of course disturbed Mrs. Rossetti, as well as Maria, but the one who suffered most was the sensitive Christina. Caught in the middle of such conflicting attitudes, she had to engage in a lifelong struggle to maintain her faith. In religion, however, as in other mat-ters, members of the Rossetti family showed remarkable tolerance and respect for the views and feelings of each other. In a way, one perhaps peculiarly Italian, each depended on the others for under-standing and love; and the only exception to such a relationship was that between Dante Gabriel and his father. Apparently Dante Gabriel's desultory way of life as a young man and his giving much of his time to reading and writing disturbed his father, who thought that his son should be applying himself assiduously to his career as an artist. His father's reproaches did little to change his son's habits, and Gabriel's affection for his father was eventually replaced by resentment.

IV *Early Reading*

When young, the children led fairly secluded lives. Except for summer visits with their maternal grandparents at Holmer Green, Buckinghamshire, they seldom traveled outside London. Few Englishmen visited the Rossettis, and rarely did the children play with other children. Continental refugees came almost nightly to talk Italian politics with their father; but, with the visitors or with politics, the children were, of course, little concerned. From an early age, they were left mainly to their own resources for most of their entertainment; and they occupied themselves with drawing, keeping notebooks, scrapbooks, "publishing" family magazines, and reading. Christina was the "least bookish of the family," according to William Michael, but among her first favorites were *The Arabian Nights*, Daniel DeFoe's *Robinson Crusoe*, and Thomas Keightley's *Classical Mythology* and *Fairy Mythology*. She then developed an interest in the Gothic tales of Charles Robert Maturin, "Monk" Lewis, and Mrs. Anne Radcliffe and in the operatic dramas of Metastasio. Among the poets, the children read Samuel Taylor Coleridge, Lord Byron, Percy Bysshe Shelley, John Keats, and Alfred Lord Tennyson. William Michael was only seven when he received a six-volume set of Shakespeare for a birthday present, but all of the children memorized and recited passages from the plays. They particularly liked *Hamlet*. Of the novelists, they preferred Sir Walter Scott, but they also read Bulwer-Lytton and Charles Dickens.

V *Works of Major Influence*

As Christina grew older, the works that most profoundly shaped her thinking were religious and philosophical; and most important to her was the Bible. Following an acquaintance through her mother's reading and teaching, she soon became thoroughly familiar with it herself and spent a lifetime studying and writing about it. She so completely immersed herself in the Bible that her own rhetorical patterns of thought are at times hardly separable from those of the Bible. In particular, she was drawn to the eschatological parts of the Bible, and of these the apocalyptic most interested her. Her favorites in the Old Testament were such Books as Isaiah, Jeremiah, Daniel, Hosea, and Amos, in which God's kingdom, a place of love and peace, is prophesied for those with faith in Jehovah. In the New Testament, she dwelt on those passages containing Jesus' promise of eternal life for his followers. But she most often turned to The Revelation of St. John the Divine and contemplated its vision of heaven for those spiritually worthy who await patiently the Day of Judgment.

Next in importance were the *Confessions* of St. Augustine and *The Imitation of Christ* by Thomas à Kempis. Christina's religious sensibility resembled Augustine's and Thomas' in her acute awareness of worldly temptations, of man's sinfulness, and of his unworthiness in God's eyes. Augustine's vivid expositions of the struggle between the forces of good and evil left a lasting impression on her, but his Christian Platonism especially appealed to her. However, she lacked Augustine's strong faith, his certainty of the directing hand of God in human affairs, and his uplifting optimism about gaining salvation and a place in the City of God.

The Imitation of Christ by Thomas à Kempis had a pervasive influence. In her life she took the path advocated by him of withdrawal from the world into the inner self as the best way of attaining sanctity. She adopted his principles of renunciation, compunction, and humility as guidelines in striving to develop the ideal Christian character. Above all, she followed him in placing her chief trust in Jesus Christ for the quieting of her restless heart and for the saving of her soul. She feared, as did Thomas, the sins of presumption and pride that often accompany an intellectual approach to Christianity. Her religion, like Thomas', was essentially one of the heart during most of her early and middle years. But from the early 1870s, almost as if she came to realize limitations in Thomas' kind of piety that was without strong doctrinal foundation, she tried to make her religion more a religion of the mind and "to relate piety . . . to revealed doctrines."[5] It was then that she wrote her most formal and doctrinal religious poetry and prose.

Two other writers that interested Christina must be mentioned: Plato and Dante. She loved Plato and often read his *Dialogues*. This interest is not surprising considering her asceticism and her preoccupation with the ideal world of the soul. She found in Plato's theory of ideas philosophical support for her religious beliefs, for it taught her to look to the unchanging form in a world of constant flux, and it strengthened her religious predilection of looking beyond the earthly to the heavenly.

In a household so devoted to Dante as was the Rossettis', Christina probably became acquainted with him fairly early, though William Michael said that she did not study him seriously until 1848. He also said that Dante was "the one poet whom she really gloried in."[6] She published in 1867 and 1884 two short articles about Dante, but her approach to the Italian poet was not that of the scholar; and, in the cryptic interpretations by her father, she had little if any interest.[7] Late in life she was to say: "I wish I too could have done something for Dante in England! Maria wrote her fine and helpful book, William's translation of the *Divina Commedia* is the best we have, and Gabriel's *Dante and his Circle* is a monument of loving labor that will outlast either. But I, alas, have neither the requisite knowledge nor the ability."[8]

Nonetheless, her reading of Dante had a significant influence on her. In her poetry, she frequently used Dantesque images and symbols; but the dominant influence was the way in which the medieval mind, as reflected in Dante, regarded reality. The phenomena of this world were thought of as giving evidence of a higher order of spiritual reality in the other world, and such a view fostered a sacramentalizing attitude. Church sacraments had both physical and spiritual aspects, and one meditated on the spiritual. In everyday life, one was expected to look beyond the merely physical and temporal to the spiritual and eternal.

The common denominator of these major works that helped form Christina's philosophy of life is their otherworldly orientation. In them, readers are urged to see the actual world as imperfect and transient, as a place of corruption and sorrow. At the same time, they are urged to envision another world, perfect and eternal, a place of ideal beauty, spiritual love, peace, and joy. As a visionary, Christina did not find it easy to ignore the distractions of this world; and, at times, her hope wavered and her vision dimmed.

CHAPTER 2

A Poet Comes Forth

IN 1842, when Christina was eleven years old, she wrote her first poem of any note, a two-quatrain birthday greeting to her mother. In that year and in the following one, she wrote several additional poems. Maria was sufficiently impressed to prophesy that Christina would be "the poet in the family." By 1844, the number increased significantly; and thereafter she seemed fully committed to poetry, though she actually composed only on impulse, as she said many times in later years. Of the poems written before she was seventeen, almost a hundred are extant; and forty-three of them appeared originally in a small volume simply titled *Verses*. Dedicated to her mother, this collection was printed on the private press of her grandfather Gaetano Polidori in 1847.

I Verses

Verses reflects Christina's early reading. The Bible, her knowledge of which was already extensive, and her mother's teaching account for the prevailing religious point of view. Individual poems give evidence of the influence of George Herbert, William Cowper, George Crabbe, William Blake, Samuel Taylor Coleridge, Percy Bysshe Shelley, John Keats, Alfred Lord Tennyson, and Robert Browning, as well as two popular women poets, Letitia Landon and Mrs. Felicia Hemans. Christina was not merely reading these poets; she was studying them and learning her art, in the way most poets do, by imitating others. It is not surprising therefore that we find little originality of conception or execution in these poems. Nevertheless, they are important because they introduce themes that interested Christina throughout her life and display techniques that became characteristic of her major poetry.

Despite the religious basis of many of the poems, the impression left is that the sentiments are not intensely felt. She is, for one thing, exhortatory. She begins not with an imagined experience or a genuine emotion but with a rhetorical concern for inculcating faith, hope, patience, or charity, and tries to establish a heavenly rather than an earthly orientation for the reader. Among the themes that continued to have special appeal for her in her later years are the transience of earthly love, joy, and beauty; the vanity of the world; the unhappiness generally experienced in life; the seeking of rest in heaven; and, in some cases, the desiring of rest in a state of dreamless sleep.

Two 1846 poems show Christina's early interest in a martyr attitude; that is, a very self-conscious accepting of the adversities of life with an almost selfish realization that God is approvingly taking note. In "The Martyr," a woman with unwavering faith goes to her death; and her soul then rises to heaven "satisfied with hopeful rest, and replete with God." In "The Dying Man to His Betrothed," a man derives a kind of pleasure from reminding his unfaithful betrothed of his suffering while he looks forward to being received into heaven. This martyr attitude turns up frequently in Christina's later poems, most often in instances where the persona's sufferings are offered to God as a means of attaining grace for salvation.

Some readers detect a note of morbidity in these early verses; and, although the note is sounded, it does not ring through the entire collection. Christina observes that life has its trials, but it also has its compensations. In "Love Attacked," written on April 21, 1846, love is thought of as fleeting, dying, and bringing heartaches. To cope with diappointment, an attitude of indifference is recommended. Two days later, she writes the palinode poem, "Love Defended," and says that, though love may bring grief, it is still worthwhile. Other poems have happy tones. In "The Rose," for example, the beautiful rose is seen as given by God "To gladden earth and cheer all hearts below." In the Shelleyan "The Song of the Star," the personified star sings contentedly of a utopian state. The most cheerful poem, "Serenade," ends with the lines, "And all is fair in earth and sky and sea. / Come, wander forth with me." Several poems, such as "On the Death of a Cat" and "To Elizabeth Read," are in the humorous vein.

The prevailing tone of the collection, however, is indeed somber as many of the titles indicate: "Burial Anthem," "The End of Time," "The Martyr," "The Dying Man to His Betrothed," "The Dead Bride," "Gone for Ever," and "The Dead City." Christina's interest in melancholy themes, with vanity, death, and frustrated love, for instance, can be explained by her poor health, by her reading of the Bible and other religious works, and by the popular poetry of the day in which these themes are prominent. But melancholy did not turn out to be merely a passing mood of a young and sensitive writer; it became for Christina a major characteristic of her disposition and poetry.

Images, for the most part, are conventional: mortals live in night, and death brings the dawning of day; the ills of the world are compared with stormy weather; clouds mean gloominess; the sun, joy; life is a "weary race," and the good life requires traveling the "narrow way."

One of the best poems in the volume is "The Dead City," probably suggested by a story in *The Arabian Nights*. The narrator tells of a journey through a lush woodland to an envisioned city in which all of the inhabitants have been turned into stone. Christina gets caught up in describing the sensuous objects along the way and in the city, forgetting, so it seems, the moral of the piece that pride and luxury cause the death of the spirit. The outstanding features, resembling those in the poetry of Keats and Tennyson, are the profusion of images and the richness of color and tone. The sometimes unskillful use of trochaic and anapestic feet, however, indicates that Christina had not yet achieved the control over meter that was to mark many of her most successful later poems.

She uses dialogue often for dialectical purposes. "Earth and Heaven," "Love Ephemeral," "Love Attacked," and "Love Defended" are representative. Though the dramatic device is often fairly rigid, she is less rhetorical in these than in other poems. She also experiments with the dramatic monologue. The colloquial language, the broken rhythms, and the liberal use of caesuras in the "Dying Man to his Betrothed" call to mind the use of these devices by Browning to achieve psychological realism.

In "Earth and Heaven," written in December, 1844, Christina is already working with the cadences that are so deftly handled in "Goblin Market." The catalog, an important feature of "Goblin Market," is used in "Earth and Heaven," in "Summer," and in other poems. Feminine rhymes, for which she retains a penchant, are common. On occasion, they produce an effect appropriate to the poem as a whole, as in "Earth and Heaven" and in "Gone for Ever"; but at times, as in "The Martyr," they are distracting and do not effectively support other elements. The simple diction and syntax, and frequent use of anaphora, alliteration, assonance, and consonance in these early verses all look forward to her later poetry.

In a brief introduction to *Verses,* her grandfather states that the "partial affection of a grandparent may perhaps lead me to overrate the merit of her youthful strains."[1] Admirers of Christina think he did not do so, for they regard the volume as a remarkable achievement for one so young. Indeed, a number of poems, mainly those composed in 1846–47, do show promise; but, on the whole, these early verses are forced; they are frequently derivative in theme, sentiment, and technique. The unsteady hand of the apprentice is struggling, with uneven success, to adapt poetic devices not yet mastered to ideas and emotions not yet deeply felt. Above all, most of the poems lack the spontaneity that characterizes her best poetry; and Christina herself thought only four of them worthy of being reprinted.

II   Maude

Perhaps the best picture of Christina on the threshold of womanhood is in *Maude,* a work of prose and verse intended as "A Story for Girls." Written sometime during 1848–50 and slightly revised in the 1870s, it was not published until 1897, almost three years after Christina's death. Though several of the poems have merit, the prose is undistinguished; and William Michael rightly regarded *Maude* as a "juvenile performance."

The loosely plotted story concerns an extremely sensitive, overly scrupulous fifteen-year-old girl, Maude Foster. She is thought clever, and her poems are handed about, but people wonder why her poetry is so "broken-hearted." One of the most revealing episodes, unquestionably autobiographical, takes place on Christmas Eve. After helping to decorate the house, Maude retires to her room with a headache, and her cousin Agnes later finds her writing in the cold. Maude is disconsolate, and she tells Agnes that she does not intend to receive communion the next morning because she feels unworthy. When Agnes remonstrates, Maude replies: "Whatever your faults may be (not that I perceive any), you are trying to correct them; your own conscience tells you that. But I am not trying. No one will say that I cannot avoid putting myself forward and displaying my verses. Agnes, you must admit so much."[2] Agnes does not. After she leaves, "Maude lay down harassed, wretched, remorseful, everything but penitent."[3]

Sometime later, following an accident, Maude dies. Agnes, who had been instructed to look after her literary remains, destroys what was obviously not intended for the public. She places a locked book of poetry in Maude's coffin. She burns other poems and fragments, but she keeps a few poems for Maude's mother. From these she makes copies of two for herself: "Fade, Tender Lily" and "What is it Jesus saith unto the soul?" Both are optimistic about the renewal of life after death.

Maude was written at an age when Christina must have felt some compulsion to make a decision about her future. Three possibilities would have occurred to her: sisterhood, marriage, or spinsterhood. Sisterhood and marriage were both considered and in time rejected, leaving spinsterhood as the only, but in many respects unhappy, alternative. In *Maude*, one of the girls joins a convent; another marries; but the author avoids the necessity of Maude's making a decision by having her die. This situation offers an interesting insight into Christina's poetry: she often turned in her poetic life to imaginative or symbolic death as an alternative to conventual life or to one in which secular love, even marriage, would play a major role. A poem, "Three Nuns," which explored attitudes related to the choice of a vocation in life, was originally part of the manuscript copy of *Maude;* but, because of a copyright problem, according to William Michael, it was excluded from the published version.[4] In a letter to William, Christina referred to "Three Nuns" as "my dreary poem," adding, "you will easily believe that, whatever other merit it lacks, it possesses unity of purpose in a high degree."[5]

Of the personal element in *Maude*, William Michael made the following summary comment:

It appears to me that my sister's main object in delineating Maude was to exhibit what she regarded as defects in her own character, and in her attitude towards her social circle and her religious obligations. Maude's constantly weak health is also susceptible to a personal reference, no doubt intentional. . . . The worst harm she appears to have done is that, when she had written a good poem she felt it to be good. She was also guilty of the grave sin of preferring to forego the receiving of the Eucharist when she supposed herself to be unworthy of it; and further, of attending musical services at St. Andrew's Church . . . instead of invariably frequenting her parish church. If some readers opine that all this shows Christina Rossetti's mind to have been at that date overburdened with conscientious scruples, of an extreme and even a wire-drawn kind, I share their opinion. One can trace in this tale that she was already an adherent of the advanced High Church Party in the Anglican Communion, including Conventual Sisterhoods. So far as my own views of right and wrong go, I cannot see that the much-reprehended Maude commits a single serious fault from title-page to finis.[6]

Some critics argue that the unflattering self-portrait in *Maude* would not be appropriate to the mature Christina. To the contrary, Maude has traits that remained constant throughout Christina's life. Among these, to name several, are her self-effacing tendency; her self-consciousness, particularly about writing poetry; her guilt feelings about actually enjoying praise for her poetic achievements; her falling into ill health at times of emotional crisis; her scrupulousness; and her religiosity. As for Christina's later poetry, specific themes in the story and verse of *Maude* continued to interest her: a preoccupation with death, a yearning for rest, a regret for the transience of beauty, and a sometimes consoling hope of salvation through Jesus.

III *The Pre-Raphaelite Brotherhood and* The Germ

Christina's first poems to come before the reading public were "Heart's Chill Between," which appeared in the *Athenaeum* on October 14, 1848, and "Death's Chill Between," which appeared in the following week's issue; and both had been written in September of the preceding year. The theme of "Heart's Chill Between" is inconstancy and of the second poem, the grief at the loss of a loved one — both common themes in her later love poetry. In technical skill and in dramatic power, both poems are superior to most of those of 1846 and 1847 that were printed in *Verses*. They adequately foretell, therefore, her development as a mature poet.

What her personal reaction was to becoming a published poet is unknown, but publication undoubtedly served as some encouragement for her to continue writing verse. Of greater encouragement was the formation in the fall of 1848 of the Pre-Raphaelite Brotherhood. Though she was not an official member, her two brothers, who were very active members, made it possible for her to associate with a group of young, enthusiastic artists and writers. The association stimulated her own literary efforts; and, when the Brotherhood began publishing a journal, Dante Gabriel saw that a number of her poems were included. Because of this close association with the Brotherhood, because her poems appeared in its journal, and because her poetry has features in common with poetry that later was called "Pre-Raphaelite," a discussion in some detail of the Pre-Raphaelite Brotherhood is necessary.

In 1848 — "towards September," says William Michael—seven young men formed what became known as the Pre-Raphaelite

Brotherhood. Holman Hunt claimed for himself and John Everett Millais the originating idea for the Brotherhood, but others have claimed it for Dante Gabriel Rossetti. This discrepancy can be explained. Before they knew Rossetti, Hunt and Millais had agreed that their own painting should represent a departure from contemporary models and the academic tradition. In Rossetti, they found not only a ready sympathizer but one who, by dint of personality, turned the departure into a minor crusade; and he urged that they establish a brotherhood. In addition to these three, the group included two other painters, James Collinson and Frederic Stephens; a sculptor, Thomas Woolner; and a government clerk, William Michael Rossetti.

At the time of its founding, the Brotherhood had no clearly articulated credo. It possessed some cohesion, however, because its members shared not only a general dissatisfaction with the state of painting in England, especially with the formalized approach of the Royal Academy, but also a youthful desire to rebel against the old order and to support a new direction that called for a commitment "to follow nature" and to achieve an individuality of expression. In short, they agreed about declaring their artistic independence. Of the thinking that loosely united members of the Brotherhood in its early days, William Michael, who served as recorder for the group, gave this account:

> Being little more than lads, these young men were naturally not very deep in either the theory or the practice of art: but they had open eyes and minds, and could discern that some things were good and others bad — that some things they liked, and others they hated. They hated the lack of ideas in art, and the lack of character; the silliness and vacuity which belong to the one, the flimsiness and make-believe which result from the other. They hated those forms of execution which are merely smooth and prettyish, and those which, pretending to mastery, are nothing better than slovenly and slapdash, or what the P.R.B.'s called "sloshy." Still more did they hate the notion that each artist should not obey his own individual impulse, act upon his own perception and study of Nature, and scrutinize and work at his objective material with assiduity before he could attempt to display and interpret it. . . .[7]

Chiefly because of Rossetti's insistence, the Brotherhood decided to publish a journal to make its views known to the public. These views initially were expressed with the graphic arts primarily in mind, but very soon, probably from the members' reading of Keats and Tennyson, they came to see that many of their "principles" applied to poetry as well. Also of importance was the great impression made on Rossetti by the poetry and visual art of Blake. In the journal, they could argue for a closer relationship among the arts, particularly painting and poetry. The first issue came out in January, 1850, with the title *The Germ: Thoughts Towards Nature in Poetry, Literature, and Art.* Of the proposed contents, the initial issue carried the following statement: "This Periodical will consist of original Poems, Stories to develope thought and principle, Essays concerning Art and other subjects, and analytic Reviews of current Literature — particularly of Poetry. Each number will also contain an Etching; the subject to be taken from the opening article of the month."[8] A brief declaration of purpose was also included: "The endeavour held in view throughout the writings on Art will be to encourage and enforce an entire adherence to the simplicity of nature; and also to direct attention, as an auxiliary medium, to the comparatively few works which Art has yet produced in this spirit."[9]

In all, only four issues of *The Germ* were published; for the first sold fewer than two hundred copies; the second, fewer than fifty. In the third issue, the title was changed to *Art and Poetry: Being Thoughts Towards Nature;* but, because sales did not increase with either it or a fourth issue, the venture was dropped. Indeed, any objective observer could have predicted an early demise for the journal. Despite an attempt by members of the Brotherhood to solicit contributions from their literary friends, only a few of the published essays and poems were of more than mediocre literary merit. More significantly, the articles dealing with artistic theory, considered individually or collectively, failed to enunciate any clear-cut, full statement of Pre-Raphaelite principles. An art manifesto was contemplated by the Brotherhood, but it was never written. Dante Gabriel's "Hand and Soul," a tale appearing in the first number of *The Germ,* did make the point that the single motive of an artist should be to look within and to paint his soul. This principle of relying on inner experience for aesthetic inspiration, with its implied insistence on artistic integrity, had particular relevance to contemporary painting; but it hardly constituted a new dogma for literature. In a modified form, however, the principle later developed into the art-for-art's sake doctrine.

One of the benefits of the publication of *The Germ* was that critics of a few leading London journals took notice of the upstart group of artists. Some of the reviews were laudatory; others were unfavorable; but the notices represented a modicum of attention for members of the Brotherhood. This recognition prepared the way for a fuller recognition, which was not to come, however, until 1853. By then, as William Michael recorded in his own journal of Pre-Raphaelite activities, "mainly owing to Millais's picture of *A Huguenot on St. Bartholomew's Eve,* the Preraphaelites had practically triumphed — issuing from the dust and smother of four years' groping surprise on the part of critics and public, taking the form mostly of thick — and — thin vituperation."[10] By this time, too, John Ruskin, the well-known and influential art critic, had already on several occasions publicly defended the Pre-Raphaelites.

But hardly had the Brotherhood achieved a measure of recognition than it ceased to exist even in an informal way. As early as 1850, James Collinson withdrew because of religious convictions; in 1852, Woolner emigrated to Australia; and, in 1853, when Millais "deserted" to become a member of the Royal Academy, the dissolution of "the whole Round Table" was complete, as Dante Gabriel wrote to Christina. No tears were shed over its breaking up; for, as serious as the young men were in their hopes for the Brotherhood, Dante Gabriel regarded it as something of a lark. Christina's lighthearted attitude toward the Brotherhood is shown in two poems she wrote in the latter part of 1853. The first, written in September before Millais' departure, celebrates the Brotherhood's achievements. The second, a sonnet written in November, celebrates its decline:

> The P.R.B. is in its decadence:
>   For Woolner in Australia cooks his chops,
> And Hunt is yearning for the land of Cheops;
>   D. G. Rossetti shuns the vulgar optic;
> While William M. Rossetti merely lops
>   His B's in English disesteemed as Coptic;
> Calm Stephens in the twilight smokes his pipe,
>   But long the dawning of his public day;
> And he at last the champion great Millais,
>   Attaining academic opulence,
> Winds up his signature with A. R. A.
>   So rivers merge in the perpetual sea;
> So luscious fruit must fall when over-ripe;
>   And so the consummated P. R. B.

Perhaps the greatest benefit of the short-lived *Germ* was that it afforded an organ of publication for the early poems of Dante Gabriel and Christina. Dante Gabriel's famous "The Blessed Damozel" was first published in its pages, and seven poems in all by Christina appeared in the journal. Her poems were unsigned, as were all contributions, in the first issue; in the second and third issues, she used the pseudonym Ellen Alleyn, suggested to her by Dante Gabriel.

To the first issue, she contributed "An End" and "Dream Land." "An End" is a plaintive lyric on the death of love. "Dream Land" has for its theme the desire for rest in death until the resurrection brings joy and peace. The latter poem is an example of her skill in using metrical regularity, alliteration, and assonance in evoking a mood. In this respect, the poem reminds one of Coleridge's "Kubla Khan" and of Tennyson's "The Lady of Shalott," poems with which she was familiar.

Three of her poems were included in the second issue. "A Pause of Thought," written in February, 1848, became in time the first part of a poem entitled "Three Stages." (The second part was written in 1849; the third, in 1854.) The poem takes the form of a dialogue of the speaker with herself and illustrates Christina's attempt to handle her themes — in this case the futile wait for love — dramatically. Her relative success with the form in "A Pause of Thought" stands in contrast to "A Testimony," which also appeared in the same issue. Almost all of "A Testimony" (written in August, 1849) consists of statements on the theme of vanity. Most readers would find the poem flat and didactic. The third poem, "Song," was originally a lyric of five stanzas in manuscript; but only the last two stanzas were published. Probably the best of her contributions to *The Germ*, it has been frequently anthologized. Its compression is particularly noteworthy:

> Oh roses for the flush of youth,
>   And laurel for the perfect prime;
> But pluck an ivy branch for me
>   Grown old before my time.
>
> Oh violets for the grave of youth,
>   And bay for those dead in their prime;
> Give me the withered leaves I chose
>   Before in the old time.

(292)

Her "Sweet Death" and "Repining" appeared in the third issue. "Sweet Death" is about another of her favorite themes, mutability: When youth and beauty die, it matters little; for rest in the Lord is "better far than these." The poem demonstrates Christina's early acquired deftness at controlling rhythm with lines of varying length. "Repining," one of her longer poems, has a narrative frame. Lamenting the emptiness of her life, a woman waits alone for the return of her lover. He finally arrives, but as a specter and is not recognized. However, when he commands her, "Rise and follow me," she does. Everywhere they travel in the world, she sees destruction and death, and always she wonders, "Why?" At last in prayer she cries out: "O Lord, it is enough, . . . / My heart's prayer putteth me to shame; / Let me return to whence I came." The woman ostensibly converses with her guide, but she is in truth holding a dialogue with her own soul about her solitary lot in life. More effective dramatizing of interior experience is to be seen in Christina's later poems. She did not republish "Repining" in her lifetime.

Precisely what Christina's literary relationship was to the Pre-Raphaelite Brotherhood cannot be easily established. She has been referred to as the "Queen of the Pre-Raphaelites," as the "high-priestess of Preraphaelitism," and as the "Jael who led their host to victory"; but these epithets hardly seem appropriate, since her role was never an active one. At no time, as mentioned, was she a formal member of the Brotherhood, though late in life she remarked to Edmund Gosse that she was the "least and last of the group." As also noted, because of the connection of her two brothers with the group, she was brought into personal touch with aspiring artists and poets, and she did find a publication outlet in their journal.

There may be little justification, therefore, for regarding Christina as a full-fledged Pre-Raphaelite, but some of her poetry and the poetry — as well as the paintings — of acknowledged Pre-Raphaelites have features in common. It has a realistic element combined with a "strangeness" or a spiritual — perhaps mystical — quality. This blend of realism and "strangeness" was noticed by a number of contemporary readers of *The Germ*. For example, Thomas Dixon, a friend of several Pre-Raphaelites, wrote to William Michael: "Why is it for these pictures and essays &c., being so realistic, yet produce on the mind such a vague and dreamy sensation, approaching as it were the Mystic Land of a Bygone Age? . . . There is [in] them the life which I long for, and which to me never seems realizable in this life."[11] In literature, these effects go back to Coleridge and Blake; for their work, as that of most Romantics and Pre-Raphaelites, represents a special attempt to unite the experiences of the senses and the spirit. It cannot be said that the Pre-Raphaelites fully succeeded; nor did Christina. For the early Pre-Raphaelites, the attempt derives in part from the moral earnestness that first motivated them, and in part from their interest, like that of their Romantic predecessors, in neomedievalism. For some of the later Pre-Raphaelites, the moral earnestness evolved into a kind of ethical aestheticism and then eventually into pure aestheticism. For Christina, the moral basis of her poetry is orthodox Christianity.

Christina and the Pre-Raphaelites were also strongly influenced by the Keats-Tennyson tradition. Among other ways, this influence showed itself in their handling of details for decorative effect and for evoking moods, in the picture-making tendency of their verse, in diction, and in metrics.

CHAPTER 3

"Goblin Market" and "The Prince's Progress"

THE Rossetti family income was so low in 1851 that Mrs. Rossetti, assisted by Christina, opened a day school at Mornington Crescent. When it did not prosper, they went to Frome, Somerset, in 1853 and began another school. Mr. Rossetti joined them, but after eleven months, with little success in the venture, they returned in March, 1854, to London to 45 Upper Albany Street, where William Michael had taken a house for the family and where Mr. Rossetti died in April. In spite of the work connected with the schools and of periods of ill health, Christina continued to write throughout the 1850s. But she managed to get only a few poems published, several of which were in Italian. Prose publications included a short story, "The Lost Titan," in *The Crayon*, an American journal, and a number of articles on Italian writers in the *Imperial Dictionary of Universal Biography*. Toward the close of the decade, she became interested in publishing a small collection of poetry in book form, but nothing immediately came of it.

I *"Goblin Market"*

Early in 1861, Dante Gabriel was busy trying to get some of Christina's poems published. He sent copies of a number of them, including "Goblin Market," to John Ruskin in hopes of getting his assistance in finding a publisher. Ruskin's reply was discouraging:

I sate up till late last night reading poems. They are full of beauty and power. But no publisher — I am deeply grieved to know this — would take them, so full are they of quaintnesses and offences. Irregular measure (introduced to my great regret, in its chief wilfulness, by Coleridge) is the calamity of modern poetry. The *Iliad*, the *Divina Commedia*, the *Aeneid*, the whole of Spenser, Milton, Keats, are written without taking a single license or violating the common ear for metre; your sister should exercise herself in the severest commonplace of metre until she can write as the public like. Then if she puts in her observation and passion all will become precious. But she must have the Form first. . . .[1]

In the meantime, Dante Gabriel interested Alexander Macmillan in her work; and three of her poems appeared in issues of *Macmillan's Magazine:* "Uphill" in February, "A Birthday" in April, and "An Apple Gathering" in August, 1861. Macmillan also agreed to publish a collection, the main poem of which would be "Goblin Market." In a letter to Dante Gabriel containing plans for the projected volume, Macmillan told of reading "Goblin Market" to a workingman's society in Cambridge. "They seemed at first," he wrote, "to wonder whether I was making fun of them; by degrees they got as still as death, and when I finished there was a tremendous burst of applause. I wish Miss Rossetti could have heard it."[2]

In March, 1862, *Goblin Market and Other Poems* was published. On the whole it was well received by reviewers and the public, although a second edition was not called for until 1865. Its success was sufficient, however, to establish Christina's reputation as one of the leading contemporary poets. Critics have noted that the recognition accorded *Goblin Market and Other Poems* was considerably greater than that gained by earlier published works of three Pre-Raphaelites: William Morris' *The Defence of Guenevere* (1858), Algernon Swinburne's *The Queen Mother and Rosamond* (1860), and Dante Gabriel's *The Early Italian Poets* (1861). Morris and Swinburne, while undergraduates at Oxford in the latter 1850s, came under the influence of Dante Gabriel Rossetti and are associated with the second phase in the historical development of the Pre-Raphaelite Movement.

The title poem of the 1862 volume, Christina's most famous poem, is the story of two sisters, Laura and Lizzie, who are tempted by goblin men to buy the luscious fruits they hawk in the glen. "Come buy our orchard fruits, / Come buy, come buy," the goblins cry. Before fleeing, Lizzie warns Laura not even to look at the evil goblins; but Laura, who cannot resist the temptation, is allowed in exchange for a golden curl to suck juices from the fruit:

> Sweeter than honey from the rock,
> Stronger than man-rejoicing wine,
> Clearer than water flowed that juice;
> She never tasted such before,
> . . . .
> She sucked and sucked and sucked the more

Fruits which that unknown orchard bore;
She sucked until her lips were sore.

(2–3)

Returning home, Laura is reproached by Lizzie and is reminded that Jeanie, a neighborhood friend, had tasted the fruit; then, unable to find the goblins again, she had died. Evening after evening Laura seeks the goblins to satisfy her craving for another taste, but she does so in vain. Finally, when Laura seems close to death, Lizzie gives the goblins a penny for fruit which she hopes to take to Laura; but they refuse, saying she must herself join them in feasting. In an attempt to force her to eat, they

> . . . cuffed and caught her,
> Coaxed and fought her,
> Bullied and besought her,
> Scratched her, pinched her black as ink,
> Kicked and knocked her,
> Mauled and mocked her,
> Lizzie uttered not a word;
> Would not open lip from lip
> Lest they should cram a mouthful in:
> But laughed in heart to feel the drip
> Of juice that syruped all her face,
> And lodged in dimples of her chin,
> And streaked her neck which quaked like curd.

(7)

In this state, she runs to Laura, who licks the juices from her face and is restored to health. The poem ends with a brief account of the sisters, now mothers, who are warning their own children to refrain from eating goblin fruit. Laura, who tells how Lizzie saved her, reminds them that "there is no friend like a sister."

As B. I. Evans observes, "the same problems are raised [by "Goblin Market"] as by *The Ancient Mariner;* a theme and movement, suggesting many things and not assignable to one source, a concluding moral acting as an anticlimax to the glamour and magic which precede it."[3] He suggests that special features of the poem can be traced to Christina's reading and to certain experiences of her life. In particular, he calls attention to similarities between "Goblin Market" and *The Arabian Nights*, William Allingham's *The Fairies*, and Thomas Keightley's *The Fairy Mythology*, all favorites of the Rossetti children. Furthermore, he notes that, besides hearing the street cries of merchants while she lived at 38 Charlotte Street, Christina would have been familiar with them from numerous written sources, especially from William Hone's *Every-Day Book*. For other influences on the poem, he mentions Christina's interest from an early age in animals and her relationship with her older sister Maria. Finally, he indicates that the concluding moral could have had its origin not only in this relationship with her sister but also, in part, in the moral advice found at the end of stories concerning sisters in *Peter Parley's Magazine*, a magazine enjoyed regularly by the Rossettis.[4]

Though William Michael wrote that he "more than once heard Christina say that she did not mean anything profound by this fairy tale,"[5] readers have always found it intriguing to probe for its allegorical and symbolic meanings. Interpretations vary, but the poem deals in its broadest outline with the theme of temptation. Laura yields to the temptation to taste the fruit offered by the goblins, an act which, because of its consequences, must be construed as evil. The fruit functions as a symbol of sin in the general biblical sense, but particularly as a sin associated with the gratification of sensual pleasures. From this sin, or fallen state, Laura is saved by her sister's sacrifice and love. On this level, the tension in the poem derives from the interplay of two forces: profane love and spiritual love. The first kind of love acts as a destroyer of man; the second, as preserver. Taking the temptation theme one stage farther, Marian Shalkhauser sees Lizzie, the redeemer, as a feminine Christ; and Laura is a combining symbol for Adam and Eve and the sinful nature of mankind generally.[6]

A. A. DeVitis relates the handling of the theme to the creative process. "The problem specifically posed by the poem," he writes, "is the nature of the experience that serves as a basis for artistic creation."[7] In Christina's case, her "art required her to have the knowledge of evil without succumbing to the corruption of evil; only by appreciating the force of evil and understanding its destructive capacity in herself could she write her poetry."[8] To Violet Hunt, the moral interpretation has a special biographical application: the poem has as its basis Maria's standing guard at night for a week to prevent Christina from eloping with James Collinson. In 1848, Collinson had proposed marriage; but Christina had declined him on grounds that he was a Roman Catholic. After reentering the Church of England, he made a second proposal and was accepted. In 1850, when he again became a Roman Catholic, Christina canceled the engagement. The event alluded to by Hunt was supposed to have taken place some nine years after their engagement had been broken and when Collinson was a married man.[9]

Lona Mosk Packer also strongly suggests that Maria is the Lizzie of the poem and that she did indeed save Christina from "spiritual backsliding." The incident, however, did not involve Collinson but William Bell Scott, a minor Pre-Raphaelite poet well known to Christina's two brothers. Scott, already married, had established an intimate relationship with a second woman, Alice Boyd, a short time before Christina wrote "Goblin Market." Maria tried to convince Christina not to continue her friendship with Scott — a friendship, according to Packer, that had been developing for some time into a serious love interest.[10] As fascinating as such a biographical interpretation is, in the absence of more substantial evidence than is now available, there is little reason for stressing it. The validity of this poem, as well as later "love" poems, rests on literary considerations; and the knowledge of such autobiographical details adds little to its impact.

Winston Weathers views the poem as prototypal of Christina's many "sister" poems in which sisters depict dramatically the struggle of various aspects of the self for "psychological integration."[11] The allurements of the goblins represent that part of the fragmented self (symbolized by Laura) which submits to sensual delight; but they also reveal, according to Weathers, a "state of mind that is escape from reality, beautiful escape at the same time it is intellectually destructive."[12] Another part of the self (symbolized by Lizzie) "must now struggle to integrate again." Lizzie "re-enacts the goblin experience, meets it face to face in a kind of therapeutic recognition, without actually succumbing to it, and by doing so is able to pull Laura back from the brink."[13] The marriage serves as a final integration of self. Since the structure of "Goblin Market" and many other poems can be examined in terms of their myth patterns, Weathers concludes that Christina Rossetti should be read "as a serious, masterful eschatological and psychological poet."[14]

At least one critic has contended that there is a discrepancy between form and meaning in "Goblin Market." The form, it is argued, is "too fast-moving and lively to allow us any serious consideration of salvation from spiritual death which the poem is really about."[15] Few concur with that judgment, for most readers find in the poem a near-perfect blending of the realistic and the imaginative, of the concrete (and pictorial) and the abstract; they see, too, a haunting rhythm adapted to serious content. These features allow the poem to function on two levels: as a fairy tale for children and as an allegory with mature intellectual appeal. Peter Quennell has remarked that "Goblin Market" is the one poem by Christina that "establishes her claim to immortality."[16]

II *"The Prince's Progress"*

In hopes of recovering her health, Christina spent three months of the winter of 1864–65 at the seashore resort of Hastings. While there, anxiously awaiting the publication of the second edition of *Goblin Market*, she worked diligently on "The Prince's Progress" and on other poems that were to comprise a second volume of her verse. She had the poems ready early in 1865; but, because Dante Gabriel delayed completing two woodcuts, publication by Macmillan of *The Prince's Progress and Other Poems* did not take place until June, 1866. In this volume, the title story, a romance, is Christina's longest poem. A few contemporary readers preferred "The Prince's Progress" to "Goblin Market," but the latter is usually considered her most successful narrative poem. Actually, Christina wrote few genuine narratives, having little inclination or skill for pure narration. Like most poets of the nineteenth century, she was more interested in a fairly expansive development of emotional states than in an economical and dramatic treatment of action or character. Frequently, however, she did use in her lyrics a narrative thread, or a "presentment of incident," as William Morris termed one of the features of Pre-Raphaelite verse. In some of the poems, a quest motif is the principal device for developing the narrative, as is the case in "The Prince's Progress."

"The Prince's Progress," originally called "The Alchemist," evolved from Christina's earlier written and published lyric, the theme of which at Dante Gabriel's suggestion was developed into the final narrative. The lyric forms part of a "bride-chaunt" sung at the end of the poem by "veiled figures" who are carrying the dead princess from the castle. The burden of the chant is a reproach to the prince for delaying too long in returning to his betrothed:

> 'Too late for love, too late for joy,
>   Too late, too late!
> You loitered on the road too long,
>   You trifled at the gate:
> The enchanted dove upon her branch

> Died without a mate;
> The enchanted princess in her tower
> Slept, died, behind the grate;
> Her heart was starving all this while
> You made it wait.'

(34)

The poem opens with a brief lament by the princess and a reply by her ladies-in-waiting that the prince has a long hard journey and that it would be better for her to dream than to weep. There follows a mystical exchange of dialogue between the prince "in his world-end palace" and the ladies. They urge him to begin:

> 'Time is short, life is short, . . .
> Life is sweet, love is sweet, use to-day while you may;
> Love is sweet, and to-morrow may fail;
> Love is sweet, use to-day.'

(26)

The long-absent prince finally starts homeward, but he soon succumbs to the temptations of a sirenlike dairymaid. Freeing himself from her allurement, he traverses a bleak and desolate country; but he eventually arrives at the cave of an aged alchemist whose years have been spent searching for the elixir of life. The prince feeds the fire and plies the bellows as the wizened man mixes a brew. While engaged in stirring, the old man dies, his fingers dipping into the liquid. His death adds the final ingredient. With a phial of the elixir for him and his bride, the prince again sets out. He is next rescued from drowning in a flooded river. Then, after dallying with his four lady rescuers, he resumes the journey but arrives too late; he is in time to see the body of the princess being carried to its burial.

The princess and the prince are less realistically conceived than the two sisters in "Goblin Market." The princess is reminiscent of Tennyson's "character-less" Mariana, and Mariana's plaintive refrain would be equally suitable to the princess' situation: " 'My life is dreary, / He cometh not,' she said; / She said, 'I am aweary, aweary, / I would that I were dead.' " The prince, the reader quickly becomes aware, is intended as an allegorical figure, an everyman, a pilgrim of life, possibly even a Christian somewhat in the mode of Bunyan's Christian in *The Pilgrim's Progress*, the work which no doubt suggested the title for Christina's poem. But the prince lacks Christian's life-likeness, his vitality, his intensity; in fact, the ineffectual prince reminds one of the medieval tableau figures in the work of Edward Burne-Jones, the Pre-Raphaelite painter. Obviously, Christina's main concern is in dramatizing the theme of self-indulgence and in evoking moods and states of mind and soul rather than in any detailed delineation of character.

"The Prince's Progress" and "Goblin Market" are among Christina's most Pre-Raphaelite poems. In both, the story functions as a parable of a moral crisis. In both, the objects, personae, and action seem to call forth specific allegorical or symbolic significance, but one finds instead a symbolic vagueness permeating the poems. In both, the approach is primarily pictorial. Details build up a richly textured and colored fabric like that of many Pre-Raphaelite paintings. In both, sensuous imagery and suggested spiritual meaning are counterpointed as in "The Blessed Damozel" and in other of Dante Gabriel's poems. In general, the techniques in "The Prince's Progress" and "Goblin Market" are like those used by Tennyson in numerous early poems that deal with spiritual or aesthetic experiences, poems such as "Mariana," "The Lady of Shalott," and "The Palace of Art."

CHAPTER 4

The Fire Burns: Desire and Frustration

ONE of the main divisions in *The Poetical Works of Christina Georgina Rossetti* (1904) is simply titled "General Poems" by its editor, William Michael Rossetti. Poems included in this section span the years from 1847 to 1893, practically all of Christina's writing life; but the majority were written during the 1850s and 1860s. Most of the poems can be deemed secular, but many have a religious context. A number of them express joy in living and a hope for future happiness that is based on faith in God and redemption, but they express more often a weakened or dead hope that brings despair and the death wish. The characteristic poems, searchingly subjective, reveal the doubts and the anguish of a troubled soul that is in conflict with the world and with itself.

William Michael's assertion that "faith with her was faith pure and absolute: an entire acceptance of a thing revealed — not a quest for any confirmation or demonstrative proof"[1] is hardly applicable to the general poems. When these poems are at all religious, they depict (with exceptions) a Christian who is crying out, like the father of the boy with an unclean spirit (Mark 9:24): "Lord, I believe; help thou mine unbelief." These storm-and-stress poems achieve an intimacy and intensity found only occasionally in the later devotional verse, and modern readers tend to regard many of them as representing Christina's highest lyric accomplishment.

The tension and suffering in these poems resulted from the imposition of a code of life — a way of thinking, feeling, and acting — that did not satisfy the needs of Christina's personality or adequately explain her experiences. The code had two major derivations, which came together as a powerful single force in her mother, a woman stronger in mind and in spirit than Christina. Because her mother was a paragon of this prescribed life, because she was ever-present, and because she was the one person to whom Christina always deferred, Christina's burden was made doubly heavy.

One of the shaping forces of this code was religious, and Christina's religious attitudes were founded on the Bible and the Book of Common Prayer. She was reared by her mother to accept unquestioningly the central tenets of Christianity and to abide rigidly by the precepts of the Church of England. According to William Michael, Christina would have characterized her own "attitude of mind" toward her faith in these words: "I believe because I am told to believe, and I know that the authority which tells me to believe is the only real authority extant, God."[2] For her, the authority of God was made known through the Bible, through the Church; and, for more than fifty-five of the sixty-four years of her life, through the guidance of her mother. But William Michael's statement again seems an oversimplification and does not suggest the true nature of her religious experience.

In a letter to Dante Gabriel, written during his final illness and at a time when he was particularly distraught, Christina alludes to two distressing periods in her own life. "However harassed by memory or by anxiety you may be," she wrote, "I have (more or less) heretofore gone through the same ordeal." She continues: "I have borne myself till I became unbearable by myself, and then I have found help in confession and absolution and spiritual counsel, and relief inexpressible. Twice in my life I tried to suffice myself with measures short of this, but nothing would do; the first time was of course in my youth before my general confession, the second time was when circumstances had led me (rightly or wrongly) to break off the practice."[3] In addition to these two critical periods during which she obviously found it difficult to submit to the teachings of the Church, she experienced other times, as her poetry gives ample evidence, when her beliefs were sorely tested and when her faith waxed for a while but then waned.

The second shaping force was societal, a force interacting closely with the religious; for the Victorian woman's identity and her place in society were narrowly and clearly defined. Socially, as well as religiously, her life was fundamentally Puritanical: her character was molded by renunciation, repression, sobriety, propriety, and piety. Social strictures were intended to support prevailing ideas about the sanctity of womanhood, marriage, and home: Queen Victoria herself served as the grand example for all women. The self-liberated woman was the exception, and she became subject to public scorn. Regarded as the moral bulwark of the family, the typical Victorian woman fought with righteousness to protect her family from the evils in the world. Christina's mother, who saw her own role in society in these terms, expected Christina to accept this role also. Christina tried desperately, but she did so at great cost to her emotional and mental stability and general happiness.

In short, the Victorian code which defined a woman's role in life, with its major religious and social dimensions, was not congenial to Christina's nature, though apparently it was for her mother and her pious sister. From her Italian father, Christina inherited strong passions and a poet's temperament; for his personal history was one of breaking away from restraining political, social, and religious institutions. His two sons, who were much like him, veered early in life from the narrow path of Victorian conventionality. It was much easier, of course, for a man to forsake the orthodox and traditional than for a woman. But her brother Dante Gabriel is proof that the rejection of one excessively inhibiting way of life can lead to another equally inhibiting and distressing — and, in his case, tragic. In Christina, who knew this possibility, it accounts, at least in part, for her forbearance and understanding of Dante Gabriel and for her compassion for him during his years of agony.

Furthermore, even allowing for society's restrictive code, Christina was constitutionally unable to engage in many activities which might have served as outlets for her intellectual and emotional energy. With an inclination toward indolence, she rarely involved herself deeply in any project. There was a feeble desire to join her aunt as a nurse at Scutari, an abortive attempt at becoming a governess, two day school failures with her mother, churchgoing, the performance of corporal works of mercy when so disposed and, when health permitted, occasional visits to relatives and friends, a few journeys, and little else. Christina's decision not to follow Maria's lead and join a sisterhood and her rejections of two marriage proposals stand out in bold relief as untaken opportunities to redirect her life. Hers was "a life," William Michael writes, "marked by . . . few external incidents."[4] Under the circumstances, one might expect her to have ordered her days around writing, but William Michael tells us that "her habits of composition were entirely of the casual and spontaneous kind, from her earliest to her latest years."[5]

I *"Rule of Avoidance"*

The clearly observable pattern of Christina's life was to withdraw from actual experience, a pattern that intensified as she got older. Her principal justification for putting aside the things of this world, for following what she called the "rule of avoidance," was religious. In a prose work, *Letter and Spirit,* published in 1883, she explained her motives:

True, all our lives long we shall be bound to refrain our soul and keep it low: but what then? For the books we now forbear to read, we shall one day be endued with wisdom and knowledge. For the music we will not listen to, we shall join in the song of the redeemed. For the pictures from which we turn, we shall gaze unabashed on the Beatific Vision. For the companionship we shun, we shall be welcomed into angelic society and the communion of triumphant saints. For the amusements we avoid, we shall keep the supreme Jubilee. For the pleasures we miss, we shall abide, and for evermore abide, in the rapture of heaven.[6]

In turning away from experience in the temporal world, Christina turned, as one sees in this passage, to the heavenly world forecast by her religion for those who are worthy. When the supernatural world provided sufficient solace, she dwelt there. When it did not, she retreated to the shadowed recesses of her psyche. But she found little there to uplift her spirit.

Retreating from life rather than becoming involved in its multiple facets had a profound effect upon the kind of poetry she wrote. On the one hand, it meant that, within a narrow stream of experiences, the emotions would be deeply felt. On the other hand, it meant that, for subject matter, she would have to rely heavily on imaginatively perceived experiences and on broad outlines of behavior. But the emotions generated by purely imagined experiences, without the re-enforcement of emotions of comparable actual experiences, are only partially satisfying. Consequently, in reading her verse one rather quickly realizes, as Elizabeth Jennings observes, that "over all her work, even the most moving," there is a "sense of something lost."[7] The "something lost" is simply but significantly much of life.

By the time she was eighteen, Christina already foresaw the direction her life would take. In "Symbols," written on January 7, 1849, the speaker asks for Christian tolerance, not wrath, when a person sees the "unfulfillment" of natural phenomena because "What if God, / Who waiteth for thy fruits in vain, / Should also take the rod?" (116). In "Endurance," dated about 1850, she argues that "I too could face death and never shrink, / But it is harder to bear hated life"; for "to suffer is more than to do." She concludes by saying that "Thousands taste the full cup," and then by asking, "Who drains the lees?" (297). The answer she knew and feared; it was a "bitter prophecy" of her life that lay ahead. And yet, knowing it, she could not or would not do anything about it.

Christina's problem, there is little doubt, became pathological or nearly so for periods in her writing career. All poetry records to some degree the unfulfilled life of its creator; but, with Christina, the degree is extreme. William Michael, of course, was well aware of Christina's withdrawal problem. In language direct and disapproving, he writes: "She was replete with the spirit of self-postponement, which passed into self-sacrifice whenever that quality was in demand."[8] He then discusses her "one serious flaw" — overscrupulosity which "made Christina Rossetti shut up her mind to almost all things save the Bible, and the admonitions and ministrations of priests."[9]

Such is the picture of Christina in the first of two sonnets grouped under the title, "A Portrait," the first poem in the "General Poems" section. Originally intended as a tribute to Saint Elizabeth of Hungary and later to Lady Isabella Howard, the poem is essentially a self-portrait:

> She gave up beauty in her tender youth,
> Gave all her hope and joy and pleasant ways;
> She covered up her eyes lest they should gaze
> On vanity, and chose the bitter truth.
> Harsh towards herself, towards others full
>   of ruth,
> Servant of servants, little known to praise,
> Long prayers and fasts trenched on her nights
>   and days:
> She schooled herself to sights and sounds
>   uncouth
> That with the poor and stricken she might make
> A home, until the least of all sufficed
> Her wants; her own self learned she to forsake,
> Counting all earthly gain but hurt and loss.
> So with calm will she chose and bore the cross
> And hated all for love of Jesus Christ.
>
>   (286)

Though written on November 21, 1850, when Christina was not quite twenty years of age, the sonnet strikes a thematic key to much of her later poetry.

A life so given to self-denial is destined to become in great measure a frustrated one. Apart from the story that the poetry tells, the "Memoir" by William Michael in *The Poetical Works of Christina Georgina Rossetti* makes it clear that Christina's life was, indeed, a frustrated one. He writes in one instance that "Her temperament and character, naturally warm and free, became 'a fountain sealed.' "[10] A recently discovered note, written by Godfrey Bilchett in his presentation copy of Mackenzie Bell's *Christina Rossetti,* indicates that, when Christina was between sixteen and eighteen, an attending physician diagnosed her illness as "a form of insanity, . . . a kind of religious mania."[11] In fact, throughout her life, her religious, social, and self-determined restraints led to an unnatural suppression of emotions and to psychic disturbances. Little wonder that William Michael should characterize "her tone of mind" as "mainly despondent."[12]

Her poetry suggests that, in order to fight her despondency and at times her despair, she considered at least three possibilities. She sought, first of all, to console herself with the expectation of her soul's salvation. For one of strong faith, this prospect can work wonders; and, on occasion, it served her well. Her faith, however, was not strong enough — contrary to commonly held opinion — to sustain her for long periods until the 1880s. She must have often felt, quite naturally, in youth and even into middle age, that the doctrine of self-abnegation, central to Christianity, was much too demanding. The best index to those times when her faith and hope were strongest are the devotional poems, but only about ten of the devotional poems included in *The Poetical Works* were written before 1850, about eighty between 1850–1865, about twenty between 1866–1879, while more than three hundred were written between 1880–1894. These are approximate figures, since the dates of most of the devotional poems cannot be precisely fixed, but relatively few of them were composed during the 1850s and 1860s when most of her general poems were written.

During these years whenever Christina's hope of redemption ebbed, she tried, as a second possible way of avoiding depression, to adopt a Stoic stance and to accept courageously her unhappy lot. But, because Stoic resignation was alien to her temperament, it was not a reliable expedient. As a third course, she often chose instead to escape the disappointments of the temporal world through imaginative wish fulfillment for sleep and death. Her most moving poems, however, are those in which she acknowledges her despondency and looks with candor at what life has been for her. Undoubtedly, she gained some therapeutic relief from suffering by giving poetic expression to it.

II *Renunciation*

The general poems trace the struggles ensuing from Christina's commitment to live a life of renunciation — to frustrate deliberately the experiences she naturally desired. In these poems, moods can be superficial; but they are frequently intense and subtly orchestrated. The best of the poems, whether the explicit and simple or the ambiguous and complex, are forceful and verge on the tragic. The renunciation theme appears early; for, even before the 1850 sonnet from "A Portrait" (quoted above), numerous poems treat it. Briefly stated, the theme is developed by a speaker who is unhappy with her life, finds the world a changing and uncertain place, and desires to withdraw from active participation in it.[13]

For example, an 1847 poem, "The Whole Head Is Sick and the Whole Heart Faint," composed when Christina was sixteen, contains the not uncommon cry of the young who see the world as distressing; but, in turning from it, they lament that "The peace of heaven is placed too high" (287). In "Have Patience" (1849), after reviewing the ages of man, the speaker concludes, "Life is weariness / From first to last — / Let us forget it" (291). This bland cry of weariness echoes through poem after poem, but its most pathetic early expression (1854) is in "From the Antique" in which the renunciation of life is complete. The desire is for nonexistence, as is seen in the opening two stanzas:

> It's a weary life, it is, she said:—
>   Doubly blank in a woman's lot:
> I wish and I wish I were a man:
>   Or, better than any being, were not:
>
> Were nothing at all in all the world,
>   Not a body and not a soul:
> Not so much as a grain of dust
>   Or drop of water from pole to pole.
>
> (312)

In the 1850s, the renunciation theme recurs frequently; indeed, it is never absent for any long period. But poems expressing varying degrees of hope are interspersed with those expressing varying degrees of hopelessness. "The First Spring Day," written in March, 1855, for instance, has for its theme the belief that "hope springs eternal in the human heart." The tone is one of the most joyful of any of the poems written in 1855; for, as spring stirs the natural world to life, the speaker in the poem exclaims: "Sing, voice of Spring, / Till I too blossom and rejoice and sing" (315). The tone changes, however, in "I Have a Message Unto Thee," written later the same month and, as Christina parenthetically notes, in sickness. "I only in my spring / Can neither bud nor sing," the speaker says; and, though the world blooms and bears fruit, she cares not "A withering crown to wear" (316–17). For solace, she turns her sights and thoughts to the eternal with God.

In the poems of renunciation, the speaker is usually aware of life and beauty in the natural world, but in October, Christina wrote "Cobwebs," a sonnet in which she depicts a barren and lifeless world, a desolate place of negation and totally devoid of hope:

> It is a land with neither night nor day,
>   Nor heat nor cold, nor any wind nor rain,
> Nor hills nor valleys: but one even plain
>   Stretches through long unbroken miles away,
> While through the sluggish air a twilight grey
>   Broodeth: no moons or seasons wax and wane,
> No ebb and flow are there along the main,
>   No bud-time, no leaf-falling, there for aye: —
> No ripple on the sea, no shifting sand,
>   No beat of wings to stir the stagnant space:
> No pulse of life through all the loveless land
>   And loveless sea; no trace of days before,
> No guarded home, no toil-won resting-place,
>   No future hope, no fear for evermore.
>
>   (317–18)

"Cobwebs" may owe something to Byron's poem "Darkness." In any case, it is a wasteland poem and, along with Browning's "Childe Roland to the Dark Tower Came," is an early Victorian example of the kind of despair poem that became fairly common in the later nineteenth and early twentieth century.

How quickly and unpredictably Christina's moods can shift is illustrated in two poems written on December 31, 1855. In one, "May," recalling the hopeful tone of "The First Spring Day," she sees life as sweet and enjoyable:

> He crowns my willing head
> With May-flowers white and red,
> He rears my tender heartseasebed:
> He makes my branch to bud and bear.
> And blossoms where I tread.

(320)

On the same day, however, she wrote "Zion Said," a devotional poem that recalls Isaiah 49:14: "The Lord hath forsaken me, and my Lord hath forgotten me." Forlorn, she pleads with the Lord:

> Open Thy bleeding Side and let me in:
> Oh hide me in Thy Heart from doubt and sin,
> Oh take me to Thyself and comfort me.

(183)

III   *"All is Vanity"*

Most often, Christina's renouncing of the world is justified on the biblical grounds of the vanity of human wishes. This vanity motif is found early and late in her verse, frequently with religious overtones. The motif derives from Ecclesiastes but is applied to her personal situation. The context, however, is not always religious. But whether considered in religious or secular terms, renunciation, though seeming a simple act, never is. Realizing this fact, Christina examines in an early poem, "Three Stages," the complexity of the attitudes and the emotional states that are associated with renunciation. The poem actually consists of three separate poems brought together under one title.

The first poem, dated February 14, 1848, deals with the difficulty, when young, of resigning oneself "utterly" to unfulfilled hope. The second, April 18, 1849, reveals the disappointment in worldly expectations and the determination that "my spirit will keep house alone" until "the last lingering chime." The third, composed more than five years after the second, speaks of the failure of any attempt to have life lapse into "a tedious monotone" because the "pulse of life" cannot be quieted. One is destined to "pursue, and yet . . . not attain" (288–90). "Three Stages" serves well as a summary of significant attitudes in Christina's philosophy of life.

Originally, the third of the linked poems in "Three Stages" was published separately under the title "Restive." This poem and two

others, "Spring" and "Acme," all written in the 1850s, were chosen
by K. E. Janowitz to illustrate Christina's treatment of the "theme of
disillusionment and loss." By detailed textual analysis, Janowitz
demonstrates how Christina "creates a vision of the self as fatally
bound to this world, by the terms of its own nature powerless to
transcend its hold and therefore doomed to destruction."[14]

From time to time, instead of outright rejection, Christina asserts
in a poem such as "To What Purpose Is This Waste" (1853) that simple faith is needed to accept the world as created. But very quickly
she reaffirms, as she does in "Next of Kin," written a month after
"To What Purpose . . . ," that the "earth is full of vanities"; and, for
her, it no longer holds any purpose, thereby precluding acceptance.
The poems on vanity range from the sweeping claim in "Vanity of
Vanities" (1847) that all pleasure and glory are vain to the certainty
that "Time will win the race he runs" with beauty in "Beauty Is
Vain" (1864) and then to the final realization that *desire* itself is the
"vanity of vanities" in "Soeur Louise de la Miséricorde" (before
1882).

The last-mentioned poem is undoubtedly autobiographical,
though ostensibly intended to refer to the woman of the title. In its
autobiographical implications, it offers a look into Christina's heart
shortly after she had turned fifty. Parts of it should be cited not only
because the vanity theme is still being repeated but also because its
emphasis has not diminished:

> I have desired, and I have been desired:
> But now the days are over of desire,
> Now dust and dying embers mock my fire . . .
> . . . .
> Oh vanity of vanities, desire!
> Stunting my hope which might have
> strained up higher,
> Turning my garden-plot to barren mire;
> Oh death-struck love, of disenkindled fire,
> Oh vanity of vanities, desire!

(411)

In tone, this poem does not differ significantly from many earlier
ones on the same theme; the same sense of futility is projected as in,
for example, the poem "She Sat and Sang Alway" of 1848:

> She sat and sang alway
>   By the green margin of a stream,
> Watching the fishes leap and play
>   Beneath the glad sunbeam.
>
> I sat and wept alway
>   Beneath the moon's most shadowy beam,
> Watching the blossoms of the May
>   Weep leaves into the stream.
>
> I wept for memory;
>   She sang for hope that is so fair:
> My tears were swallowed by the sea;
>   Her songs died on the air.
>
>   (290)

IV *Stoicism*

The theme in "She Sat and Sang Alway" has considerable force
because it is developed with an emotional restraint that has the
overall effect of suggesting a Stoic's impassivity toward life. Other
poems also suggest that Christina tried to avoid the depression that
accompanies confusion and negativism by assuming a Stoic attitude,
one that she early in life admired in "Lady Montrevor" (1848).
Referring to a heroine from a Maturin novel, the sonnet praises the
fortitude of the speaker in bearing adversities. Dissatisfaction with
the condition of life brings not regret but courageous resignation:

> And, though young spring and summer pass away,
>   And autumn and cold winter come again,
> And though my soul, being tired of its pain,
>   Pass from the ancient earth, and though my clay
> Return to dust, my tongue shall not complain. . . .
>
>   (290)

At its best, this Stoic voice has something of the clarion ring found in
Emily Brontë's poetry: but Christina could be the Stoic only with
great difficulty. As her life and as most of her poetry attest, she
lacked the temperament, the strength, and the courage needed to
live the Stoic's ideal of resignation and self-dependence; that is, to
live dispassionately or without at least some glimmer of hope of
future fulfillment for her longings. Because much of Christina's
poetry deals with the self-consciousness of suffering rather than with

the dramatic presentation of suffering itself, the reader tends to regard her with sympathy rather than with admiration.

In a poem like "Endurance," already referred to as an example of Christina's "rule of avoidance," her attempt at being Stoical degenerates into the rationalization of frustration and unhappiness:

> Yes, I too could face death and never shrink.
>   But it is harder to bear hated life;
> To strive with hands and knees weary of strife;
>   To drag the heavy chain whose every link
> Galls to the bone; to stand upon the brink
>   Of the deep grave, nor drowse tho' it be rife
> With sleep; to hold with steady hand the knife
>   Nor strike home: — this is courage, as I
>   think.
> Surely to suffer is more than to do.
>   To do is quickly done: to suffer is
> Longer and fuller of heart-sicknesses.
>   Each day's experience testifies of this.
> Good deeds are many, but good lives are few:
>   Thousands taste the full cup; who drains
>   the lees?
>
>   (297)

For the truly Stoical, she sometimes substitutes an attitude approximating indifference, as in "Remember" (1849), "The Last Look" (1855), and with particular effectiveness in this earlier written (1848) and justly celebrated lyric, "When I am Dead, My Dearest":

> When I am dead, my dearest,
>   Sing no sad songs for me;
> Plant thou no roses at my head,
>   Nor shady cypress tree:
> Be the green grass above me
>   With showers and dewdrops wet:
> And if thou wilt, remember,
>   And if thou wilt, forget.
>
> I shall not see the shadows,
>   I shall not feel the rain;
> I shall not hear the nightingale
>   Sing on as if in pain:
> And dreaming through the twilight

> That doth not rise nor set,
> Haply I may remember,
> And haply may forget.
>
> (290–91)

Though her indifferent and her Stoic attitudes tend to curb the display of excessive emotion. Christina possesses a strong sense of poetic tact, one which rarely permits her to be mawkish. There is no wringing or writhing, no effusion of uncontrolled emotion; for her usual practice is to render feeling through terse statement and spare imagery, as she does in "When I am Dead, My Dearest." Another fine illustration is in the previously quoted "Oh Roses for the Flush of Youth" (1849).

V "It Passed Away"

The theme of "Oh Roses for the Flush of Youth" is a lament over growing old before one's time, of not making the most of life. Christina broods over this thought frequently in poems composed around 1849. Indeed, the theme reoccurs in almost every period. The sentiment of the concluding stanza to "May," written in November, 1855, for example, is not essentially different from that expressed in poems on the theme written earlier or later:

> I cannot tell you what it was;
> But this I know: it did but pass.
> It passed away with sunny May,
> With all sweet things it passed away,
> And left me old, and cold, and grey.
>
> (318)

Occasionally, however, the depression of spirit that comes with realizing that one has not made the most of life gives way to a lighter tone. "Another Spring" (1857) is one such instance in which the speaker, musing over the thought, "If I had the chance again," admits that she would adopt a *carpe diem* philosophy:

> If I might see another Spring,
>   I'd not plant summer flowers and wait:
> I'd have my crocuses at once,
>   My leafless pink mezereons,
> My chill-veined snowdrops, choicer yet
>   My white or azure violet,

> Leaf-nested primrose; anything
>   To blow at once, not late.
>
> If I might see another Spring,
>   I'd listen to the daylight birds
> That build their nests and pair and sing,
>   Nor wait for mateless nightingale;
> I'd listen to the lusty herds,
>   The ewes with lambs as white as snow,
> I'd find out music in the hail
>   For all the winds that blow.
>
> If I might see another Spring —
>   Oh stinging comment on my past
> That all my past results in 'if' —
>   If I might see another Spring
> I'd laugh to-day, to-day is brief;
>   I would not wait for anything:
> I'd use to-day that cannot last,
>   Be glad to-day and sing.
>
> (333)

With only a few poetic exceptions, the intention is never fulfilled; and the typical poem on the theme of a wasted life expresses gloom with implied or stated regret.

VI *Death Wish*

By the time Christina is in her thirties, the unfulfilled life theme generally merges with the more inclusive death-in-life theme. The emptiness, the unfruitfulness, of her life haunts her; and her only hope is for death, as in this excerpt from "An 'Immurata' Sister" (c. 1865):

> Men work and think, but women feel;
>   And so (for I'm a woman, I)
> And so I should be glad to die,
>   And cease from impotence of zeal,
> And cease from hope, and cease from dread,
>   And cease from yearnings without gain,
> And cease from all this world of pain,
>   And be at peace among the dead.
>
> (380)

Christina's dedication to a life of self-abnegation, bringing with it emotional frustration and psychological strain, explains, to a great extent, her preoccupation with thoughts of death. Ill health, real or imagined, that plagued her throughout life also played a part in her believing that the specter of death was ever near. Whatever the basis, and whether death is regarded in religious or secular terms, symbolic or literal, it is one of the prominent themes in Christina's poetry. In fact, more than four hundred fifty poems are concerned in some way with death.

The year 1849 and the early months of 1850 — the time during which Christina wrote *Maude* — must have been particularly trying, for in a great number of poems of that period the plea is uttered for sleep and death (terms often used synonymously) as an escape from suffering and weariness. The pathetic cry is heard over and over: "Rest, rest, a perfect rest" ("Dream Land"); "O Earth, lie heavily upon her eyes; / Seal her sweet eyes weary of watching, Earth" ("Rest"); "Sleep, let me sleep, for I am sick of care; / Sleep, let me sleep, for my pain wearies me" ("Looking Forward").

In some poems, the place of rest is like a twilight zone where the person, though presumed dead, nonetheless possesses varying degrees of consciousness; but the emotional responses are so limpid that they do not disturb the sought-for rest. In "After Death" (1849), which depicts such a state, the speaker, a dead woman, describes the last visit of the man she loves to view her corpse. She hears him and is aware of his reaction, but her own terse response is limited:

> He did not love me living; but once dead
>   He pitied me; and very sweet it is
> To know he still is warm though I am cold.

(293)

This matter-of-fact tone to which Christina often resorted prevents the note of self-pity from cloying.

Aside from the poems in which one passes from death to a twilight zone of rest, either as a permanent or as a temporary state, most of the "death" poems can be broadly classified as presenting two views: death as an end of all life or death as leading to an after-life. These views are set forth in a single poem in 1850, "Two Thoughts of Death." In the first of two sonnets that comprise the poem, the speaker argues that the dead girl is indeed dead and that other living forms may derive sustenance from her corrupted body. In the second sonnet, she argues for the immortality of the girl's soul; but such expressions are common, as one would expect, among Christina's devotional poetry. Of those among the general poems, the context is less doctrinal, the tone is much less prayerful, but the expectation of a happy after-life is treated with traditional Christian optimism, as in the closing of "We Buried Her Among the Flowers" (1850):

> So she sleeps hidden in the flowers;
>   But yet a little while,
> And we shall see her wake and rise,
>   Fair, with the self-same smile.
>
> (301)

During the same years that Christina was writing poems expressing hope in a Christian resurrection, however, she was also writing poems saying that death ends life. Of course, both views on death are conventionalized in Western culture; but the interesting point about their manifestation in Christina's poetry is the suddenness of the shifts. These shifts can be accounted for, in great part, by the uncertainty of Christina's attitudes and by the instability of her emotions. When hope appears strongest, it then fades quickly or is entirely lost; and the speaker is engulfed by doubts. For example, on May 15, 1849, she writes the poem "Rest" in which death is viewed as an interim period until the "morning of Eternity"; then a few weeks later on June 8, she writes in "Looking Forward" that the soul does not survive after death but that immortality of a sort is achieved when the dust of the deceased combines with the soil and nourishes flowers. Death brings life only in the natural, not in the supernatural world.

Thus in the 1850s and into the mid-1860s, she is writing some poems in which death is the ultimate end and some in which death is the prelude to heaven. But with whichever significance, the death wish continues as a theme throughout her poetry. A poetry so preoccupied with death indicates, in general, the poet's failure to find sufficiently meaningful most of the activities that occupy the average individual. Abnegation followed naturally, with different emotional overtones.

An important change in tone occurs in some of the "death" poems in the 1860s. Many early "death" poems are charged with a strong emotional rejection of life, and the accompanying pain and unhappiness are keenly felt. But in a poem like "Life and Death" (1863), for example, much of the tension is gone and the tone of resignation is almost limp:

> Life is not sweet. One day it will be sweet
> To shut our eyes and die.
>
> (358)

So it is in "A Smile and a Sigh" (1866), in "Of My Life" (1866), and in other poems of the 1860s, as well as in many of those of the 1870s and 1880s. Three poems of the two last-mentioned decades are additional illustrations of this changed tone. "Mirrors of Life and Death" (before 1878), with its closing line, "I hope, and I abide," expresses a weakened hope but also a toleration simply for what remains of life. "To-Day's Burden" (about 1880) points out the "restlessness" of life for all and the impossibility of having it otherwise. "Passing and Glassing" (before 1882), which acknowledges the inevitability of death, concludes:

> All things that pass
>   Are wisdom's looking-glass;
> Being full of hope and fear, and still
>   Brimfull of good or ill,
> According to our work and will;
>   For there is nothing new beneath the sun;
> Our doings have been done,
>   And that which shall be was.
>
> (411)

These poems are more philosophical and less dramatic than earlier ones about the same themes. Most earlier poems are developed by counterpoint: a passionate desire for death is accompanied by an almost equally passionate fear of, and reluctance to accept, death. In later poems, in contrast, almost all passion is dissipated; and death is accepted existentially as the ultimate reality of life. This attitude is Christina's prevailing one about death in the secular poems as she moves into her final writing years, most of which, however, are devoted to religious compositions.

VII Love

Though the death wish may be evoked by many different experiences, its most poignant evocation is likely to follow the frustration of love, especially that between man and woman with its anticipated sexual consummation. Love is central to a person's sense of fulfillment in life; its frustration or outright rejection, for whatever reasons, can quickly lead to a general renunciation of life and consequently to the death wish. In a metaphorical sense, death becomes a suitor and even a bridegroom substituting for the earthly lover and bridegroom. The death theme, therefore, often functions conjunctively as a love theme. The love theme, however, is complex and has a variety of manifestations in Christina's poetry.

From the beginning, there is the longing for love and the acknowledgment of the primacy of its need. The effect on one of loving is glorifying, even when the love is not returned. In "A Pause" (1853), the speaker is a dead girl, or one who is about to die, whose "thirsty soul" cannot be released from the body because her own love was unrequited; therefore, she waits for the coming of the man she loves. Her only awareness is of him; and, as he approaches, she says: "Then first my spirit seemed to scent the air / Of Paradise . . . ; and I felt my hair / Put on a glory, and my soul expand" (308). Possibly the awaited lover is an allegorical figure for Christ, but Christina treats him as an earthly lover. In any case, the main quality of this desired love is spiritual — platonic or idealized. This idealization of love, as Christina saw in Dante's *Vita Nuova*, was one way of rendering love passionless; or, from another and seemingly contradictory point of view, it was a way of expressing passion for an experience which by definition was without passion. In poem after poem, whether indirectly or directly expressed, the hope for an ideal love persists:

> Give me the flame no dampness dulls,
> > The passion of the instinctive pulse,
> Love steadfast as a fixèd star,
> > Tender as doves with nestlings are,
> More large than time, more strong than death:
> > This all creation travails of —
> She groans not for a passing breath —
> > This is Forget-me-not and Love.
> > > ("A Bed of Forget-Me-Nots," 323)

These lines were written in 1856, but the concept of an earthly love elevated to heavenly spirituality was adopted early and was not totally forsaken until fairly late. That it was unattainable in life, and therefore in a sense dead, she realized when only eighteen, for she wrote in "An End":

> Love, strong as Death, is dead.
> Come, let us make his bed
> Among the dying flowers. . . .
>
> He was born in the spring
> And died before the harvesting. . . .
>
> (292)

Though sixteen years later she reaffirms in "Dead Hope" that "Hope dead lives nevermore, / No not in heaven," she did hope in her early years that love unfulfilled in this world might be fulfilled in the next. Two 1858 poems dramatize her decision to forsake earthly love for later spiritual fulfillment in heaven. In "The Convent Threshold," a woman, sharing an unnamed sin with her lover, pleads with him to repent as she has done. Envisioning herself in paradise but still longing for him, she says his repentance will mean that "There we shall meet as once we met, / And love with old familiar love."

In the second poem, "From House to Home," the rejection is of all earthly pleasures. At first the speaker built (not unlike the speaker in Tennyson's "The Palace of Art") "a pleasure-place within my soul; / An earthly paradise supremely fair / That lured me from the goal" (21). But, heeding the call of the spirit and being promised that she and her lover will "meet again . . . in a distant land," she undergoes the suffering and cleansing of purgatory and finally gains heaven, where she awaits her beloved. In reference to both of these poems, Packer observes that "the solution ignores the human lover. In soaring, Christina turns her back upon the earthly responsibilities of relationship which require action and decision here on this earth."[15]

The decision to forsake earthly love is also, as one would expect, part of the broader rejection of the world because of her belief, however wavering, that all things of the world are vain. This belief is closely allied to the belief that a first priority claim is made upon her as the bride of Christ to whom her life must be dedicated. Death for her could open the door to love and to a new life because with death came the possibility of union with Christ. Such thinking was related to the dichotomy concept of body and soul still prevalent in the Victorian mind, and it had serious social implications. Since sensual and sexual experiences were tainted because they appealed to the baser nature of man, the denial of these experiences was regarded as an act that brought a person closer to the Godhead, that made one Christ-like and therefore worthy of salvation.

But the conflict between secular and divine love was never satisfactorily resolved for Christina. She could not completely resign herself to the loss of the human-love experience. At the same time that "The Convent Threshold" is, as Alice Meynell notes, "a song of penitence for love," it "yet praises love more fervently than would a chorus hymeneal."[16] The cry, "My heart is breaking for a little love" ("L.E.L.," 1859), is uttered repeatedly. The hope and regret persist through most of her life. Full of misery, with "soul . . . crushed and like to die," the speaker in "If I Had Words" (1864) still seeks love:

> If I had wings as hath a dove,
> I would not sift the what and why,
> I would make haste to find out Love,
> If not to find at least to try.
>
> (371)

Though she continues to write such love-quest poems, she also continues to claim that love is dead, as she does, for example, in "In a Certain Place" (1866). While proclaiming love's death in this poem, however, she still wonders whether, even if love were alive, she would "know him." Six years later she admits in "Love Lies Bleeding" that she never really knew love.

As late as 1876 the hope for romantic love is still heard in "A Bride Song," "Confluents," and "Bird Raptures"; but, by this time, the desire is almost passionless. Appropriately in "Bird Raptures," the nightingale, a bird of sorrow, of lament, of hopeless love, becomes a symbol of her lifelong quest:

> O herald skylark, stay thy flight
> One moment, for a nightingale
> Floods us with sorrow and delight.
> To-morrow thou shalt hoist the sail;
> Leave us to-night the nightingale.
>
> (391)

While desiring love, Christina also feared it; and her fear was derived in part from her religious attitudes and in part from her psychological make-up. She realized of course that temporal love was fraught with uncertainties and sorrow. Consequently, most of her love poetry is concerned with anxiety and unhappiness.

Unfaithfulness in love is a common theme. A fairly early strong statement of it appears in "Two Parted":

> 'Sing of a love lost and forgotten,
>   Sing of a joy finished and o'er,
> Sing of a heart core-cold and rotten,
>   Sing of a hope springing no more.'
> 'Sigh for a heart aching and sore.'
>
>   (309–10)

The speaker says, "I was most true and my own love betrayed me, / I was most true and she would none of me" (310). Though the lament in the poem is by a man, Christina may well have been reliving her own experience with James Collinson in 1850. Overscrupulous as she was, she probably felt some guilt about having broken the engagement, the guilt lingering the three years to 1853, when this poem was written.

The situation is reversed in "The Hour and the Ghost" (1856). Haunted by the past, a bride hears the ghost of her rejected lover bid her to forsake her husband and to come away with him to "crown our vows." The bride, pleading with the bridegroom to "Forget not as I forgot," is compelled to join the ghost, who warns in the concluding lines of the poem that

> Thou shalt visit him again
> To watch his heart grow cold:
> To know the gnawing pain
> I knew of old. . . .
>
>   (327)

In "Light Love" (1856), the man deserts the woman who bore his child and who still loves him. In "Maude Clare," the woman is given up for another bride. In these poems, as in a number of others, the vows exchanged between the lovers were expected to be binding forever; and, when broken, some bitterness is felt by the one forsaken. In "Last Night" (1863), however, the forsaken, though not without some regret, advises the one who took her place to make the most of her opportunity for love. By 1882, in "Brandons Both," when the lover leaves one cousin for another, the forsaken one feels no bitterness at all. Christina seems to have moved to a more realistic acceptance of the vicissitudes of love.

Along with poems of broken vows, are those in which love is unrequited and in which little or no emphasis is placed on the "once-we-loved" motif. "Cousin Kate" (1859) tells the story of a maiden who gave her love to a nobleman who preferred to marry her cousin. "Margery" (1863), which relates the sorrow of a girl who gave her love but did not have it returned, offers a particularly interesting insight into the Victorian code governing the relationship between the sexes. The suitor apparently rejected the girl because she "let him know she loved him so!" "Girls should not," the reader is told, "make themselves so cheap." Christina also points out in "Husband and Wife" (1865) that even in marriage one may love but not the other.

Separation of lovers is also a common theme, but in some poems the reason for the separation is ambiguous. Usually, the separation necessarily follows from the decision to renounce earthly love in the hope of spiritual love fulfillment in heaven. Such is the case in "The Convent Threshold," in "From House to Home," and in the later sonnet sequence, "Monna Innominata."

The degree of hope of being reunited varies but is generally strong enough to give an optimistic tone to the poem. In quite a few poems, however, hope is minimized. In "Songs in a Cornfield" (1864) and in "A Fisher-Wife" (before 1882), for example, Christina prefers to stress the pangs of separation, the longing, and the melancholy. And in a number of poems no hope for reunion is given, as, for instance, in "One Foot on Sea, And One on Shore" (before 1882). The parting in these poems is attributable to unspecified circumstances in life. Lovers will meet and part, meet and part again any number of times, but the separation caused by death most often figures in the love poems that end with the hope of heavenly reunion. The last stanza of "Meeting" (1864) gives the usual pattern, one that becomes a refrain in many other poems:

> To meet, worth living for:
> Worth dying for, to meet.
> To meet, worth parting for:
> Bitter forgot in sweet.
> To meet, worth parting before,
> Never to part more.

(366)

But not all love continues after death. There comes a time, the male speaker says in "Long Looked For" (1854), "When life and love are finished / And even I forget" (313). In "The Poor Ghost" (1863), a ghost rebukes his former lover for disturbing his rest: "Life is gone," he says, "Then love too is gone" (360). In the Hardyesque "A Bird's Eye View" (1863), the bride dies at sea; and the bridegroom soon forgets her and marries another. This realistic view is not uncommon among Christina's love poems, but the undertone of irony in this poem is rare.

The love dealt with in Christina's poems seldom has any immediate actuality in the context of the poem, and past love often becomes indistinguishable from a dreamed love. Since past love — and that unfulfilled — is only a memory, it can be given a semblance of reality only as a dream; that is, be called forth by the imagination. Poems of past and dreamed love are numerous in the 1850s, and among these are "Song" (1851), "What?" (1853), "Dream Love" (1854), "Long Looked For" (1854), "Echo" (1854), and "For One Sake" (1857).

The appropriately titled poem "Echo" contains the characteristic features of the dream poems. In the first stanza, the speaker, addressing her lover, calls for his return in a dream; but she realizes that he is no more than a "memory, hope, love of finished years." In the second stanza, the bittersweet aspect of the relationship is recalled as is the once-held hope that the love might have been fulfilled in heaven. In the last stanza, she reiterates her desire for a vicarious love experience in a dream:

> Yet come to me in dreams, that I may live
>   My very life again though cold in death:
> Come back to me in dreams, that I may give
>   Pulse for pulse, breath for breath:
> Speak low, lean low,
>   As long ago, my love, how long ago.
>
> (314)

The dream or imaginative experience serves as a palliative for frustrated love. But, from time to time, Christina forsakes the dream world to face her real mental and emotional state; and she then engages in what Matthew Arnold called "the dialogue of the mind with itself." Momentarily freed, the "locked-in ego" is allowed to speak, as in "Introspective," one of Christina's most distressing poems. Dated June 30, 1857, the poem alludes to an event that somehow brought ruin and then terrible suffering in its aftermath. Like a hammer, the opening stanza measures out the emotion:

> I wish it were over the terrible pain,
> Pang after pang again and again:
> First the shattering ruining blow,
> Then the probing steady and slow.
>
> (331)

"Up I stand," says the speaker, "like a blasted tree / By the shore of the shivering sea." The cause of her ruin is to remain a secret, being revealed only to her soul: "O my soul, I talk with thee, / But not another the sight must see." In the closing stanza, she reasserts the Stoic's fortitude:

> I did not start when the torture stung,
> I did not faint when the torture wrung:
> Let it come tenfold if come it must,
> But I will not groan when I bite the dust.
>
> (331)

As is usual in the previously discussed Stoic poems, the reader feels here, too, that she is less able to bear the suffering than the rhetoric suggests. Nevertheless, the suffering is genuine even though the ending does not adequately resolve the emotional crisis.

As already noted, Stoicism never proved a satisfactory answer to Christina's problems, and escape into a dream world proved at best a temporary expedient. The possibility that remained was to fall back upon her faith; and, when strong, it gave her some comfort and made her burden bearable. Apparently this situation occurred on June 30, for on the same day that she wrote "Introspective," she wrote, and in all probability later rather than earlier, "A Better Resurrection," a devotional poem. The faith that helped her control her despair seemingly helped her control its poetic expression, for "A Better Resurrection" is more skillfully written than "Introspective."

Each stanza of "A Better Resurrection" stresses the desolation of the speaker but ends with a plea to Christ for regeneration:

> I have no wit, no words, no tears;
>   My heart within me like a stone
> Is numbed too much for hopes or fears.
>   Look right, look left, I dwell alone;
> I lift mine eyes, but dimmed with grief
>   No everlasting hills I see;

My life is in the falling leaf:
O Jesus, quicken me.

My life is like a faded leaf,
My harvest dwindled to a husk:
Truly my life is void and brief
And tedious in the barren dusk;
My life is like a frozen thing,
No bud nor greenness can I see;
Yet rise it shall — the sap of Spring;
O Jesus, rise in me.

My life is like a broken bowl,
A broken bowl that cannot hold
One drop of water for my soul
Or cordial in the searching cold;
Cast in the fire the perished thing;
Melt and remould it, till it be
A royal cup for Him, my King:
O Jesus, drink of me.

(191–92)

The imagery of the first two stanzas is not memorable; but the simple syntax, diction, and the strong iambic cadence give considerable intensity to the emotional values. Then in the last stanza, a distinctive simile, suggested by the broken bowl image in Ecclesiastes (12:6), effectively climaxes the movement from grief to hope in Christ.

Less than five months after composing "Introspective" and "A Better Resurrection," Christina wrote on November 18, 1857, "A Birthday," a poem unmatched in its exhilaration by anything else she ever wrote. No biographical explanation has satisfactorily accounted for its joyousness, but it has been a favorite with readers since its publication:

My heart is like a singing bird
Whose nest is in a watered shoot:
My heart is like an apple-tree
Whose boughs are bent with thickset fruit;
My heart is like a rainbow shell
That paddles in a halcyon sea;
My heart is gladder than all these
Because my love is come to me.

> Raise me a dais of silk and down;
>   Hang it with vair and purple dyes;
> Carve it in doves and pomegranates,
>   And peacocks with a hundred eyes;
> Work it in gold and silver grapes,
>   In leaves and silver fleurs-de-lys;
> Because the birthday of my life
>   Is come, my love is come to me.

(335)

The pictorial quality and the rich texture are Pre-Raphaelite features. The first of two sets of images associates the speaker's joy with objects of nature; the second set, with an artistically embellished royal dais.[17] Parallel rhetorical structure produces in two stages an accumulating effect of joy. An initial high point comes at the end of the first stanza, and a final crescendo of emotion appears at the end of the second stanza. The strongly accentuated iambics, with minimal variation, and the octosyllabic lines give force and rapidity of movement appropriate to the speaker's exuberance. The trochaic feet which open four lines of the last stanza add thrust to the intensifying tone. All the poetic elements fuse to capture what was one of the rare moments of sheer delight in Christina's poetic life.[18]

But only five days later Christina returned in "An Apple Gathering" to the dual theme of broken friendship and of action that bore no fruit. She returned, too, to a somber mood; the note of regret in the poem contrasts sharply with the gladness of "A Birthday." On the same day as "An Apple Gathering" she also wrote "Winter: My Secret," a poem in which she may be recalling the secret — undoubtedly pertaining to love — of "Memory, I" (November 8, 1857) and "A Nightmare" (September 12, 1857), and perhaps the "ruin" of "Introspective." But "Winter: my Secret" is very different in tone from these gloomy poems. This dramatic monologue strikes a delicate balance between seriousness and playfulness. The opening line establishes the impression of listening in on a conversation already underway: "I tell my secret? No indeed, not I." Several times the speaker is on the verge of revealing the secret but prefers to tease the inquisitor, even suggesting that there may be "no secret after all." Finally, she ends by saying that in summer "Perhaps my secret I may say, / Or you may guess" (366).

This playful handling of a love theme is unusual. Most often it is treated seriously with explicit indications or intimations that the love is sinful. The reason will generally be vague, though frequently love seems sinful simply because it is human. In "The Convent Threshold," the guilt accompanying sinful love is openly expressed. The woman speaker in the poem urges her lover to repent and to look forward to spiritual love fulfillment in heaven. In this poem, the answer to the rejection of earthly love proves emotionally satisfying. But, as has been seen, in other poems, such as "A Nightmare" and "Introspective," the problem does not admit of an external solution; and the consequences are psyche-shattering.

To dramatize the fragmenting effect on the mind of an unfulfilled love experience and to try to effect an integrating of the ego, Christina wrote a number of "sister" poems. In these, two, three, or four sisters represent different aspects of the split personality that was caused by conflicting attitudes and mixed emotions toward love. The structure in these poems allows for more psychological penetration and subtlety than in the conventional love lyrics in which one speaker expresses her feelings or in the dialogue poems of lover and beloved or even in the dramatic monologues.

Her most interesting and best-known "sister" poem is "Goblin Market," a powerful enactment of the separating and reintegrating of the ego. The happy reuniting of the sisters and their individual fulfillment of love in marriage in this poem occurs also in "Maiden Song" (38–41). Two sisters, Meggan and May, separate from a third, Margaret, and by their singing attract husbands. Margaret's singing not only wins her a royal husband but it brings "her sisters home / In their marriage mirth." However, most of the "sister" poems do not end happily. In "Sister Maude," one of the sisters condemns another for telling their parents of her love. In "Noble Sisters," a woman turns away her sister's lover, cursing her for shaming their father's name. In "The Ghost's Petition" and in "Songs in a Cornfield," no antagonism exists between the sisters but there is a significant difference in their psychic states. In "The Ghost's Petition," one sister is undisturbed; but the other is deeply distressed as she awaits her husband's arrival. He does return but as a spirit from the dead who points out that he has no need of her in his world. This view is opposed to that in numerous love poems in which a reuniting of separated lovers is anticipated in the spiritual world. In "Songs in a Cornfield," three sisters sing joyfully in their work, presumably because they do not have false lovers. A fourth sister, despairing of her lover's return, sings a song contemplating death.

At times, when Christina felt that her hopes for love were shattered or — and this is probably what counted most in her inner life — when she failed to formulate a psychologically acceptable attitude toward love, she turned to God, the ready answer seemingly to her dilemma. This turning away from unhappy earthly love to the love of God is told in many poems. The common pattern of action is clearly seen in "Twice" (1864) in which, having had her heart broken by a lover, the speaker simply gives it to God to be renewed. In her dissatisfaction with the quality of earthly love, indeed, with life generally, Christina could decide easily enough to look to God; but she always keenly realized that fulfillment in God meant a long and arduous journey, as is seen in "Up-Hill" (1858):

> Does the road wind up-hill all the way?
>   Yes, to the very end.
> Will the day's journey take the whole
>   long day?
>   From morn to night, my friend.
>
> (339)

The "downhill path is easy," she warns in a contrasting poem, "Amor Mundi" (1865), "but there's no turning back." This fear of having no opportunity to turn back, once started downhill, was one of the great fears of Christina's life. With her "wiredrawn scrupulosity," she was at times uncertain about whether she was traveling uphill or downhill.

In the 1860s and early 1870s, Christina found it difficult to push temporal thoughts from her mind for long and to keep her eye focused on the gleam of heavenly visions. Even though she succeeded in avoiding involvement in worldly affairs — living more and more the life of a recluse as she became older — she still looked within to the recesses of her memory; and she did so with regrets. Already by 1865 in "From Sunset to Rise Star" she writes:

> For I have hedged me with a thorny hedge,
>   I live alone, I look to die alone.
> Yet sometimes when a wind sighs through
>   the sedge
>   Ghosts of my buried years and friends
>   come back,
> My heart goes sighing after swallows flown
>   On sometime summer's unreturning track.
>
> (375)

The following year (1866), in poems like "An 'Immurata' Sister," "In a Certain Place," and "Cannot Sweeten," she continues to grieve over the emptiness of her life because she had never fully experienced love. And she again looks heavenward with some hope as in "They Desire a Better Country" and in "Meeting," but she remains distressed throughout the 1870s over the inability of lovers to achieve harmony ("An Echo from Willow-Wood") or of lovers to consummate their love ("Love Lies Bleeding"). Occasionally, a poem deals with a resuscitated, albeit faint, longing for love, such as in "A Bird Song" and "A Bride Song"; but there is always the melancholy note that cannot be suppressed of the unlikelihood of ever truly loving. With the almost total loss of hope for love went one of Christina's main inspirations for composition, and by 1874 she confessed to Alexander Macmillan, her publisher, that "the fire has died out, it seems; & I know of no bellows potent to revive dead coals."[19]

VIII *"Sleeping at Last"*

During the same period in poems on the vanity theme, the attitude of the speaker becomes almost apathetic:

> Morrow by morrow
>   Sorrow breeds sorrow,
> For this my song sigheth;
>   From day to night
> We lapse out of sight. —
>   Such is life that dieth.

("Days of Vanity," 388)

Life and death are contemplated dispassionately; for, as always, she sees "The mystery of Life, the mystery / of Death . . . / Darkly as in a glass" ("Mirrors of Life and Death"). That the beautiful and the ordinary, the good and the bad, indeed, that all things move irreversibly toward death she can now accept philosophically. But what does it all mean? After a lifetime of uncertainty and unhappiness, she still is in doubt and confusion. "The whole earth," she asserts in "Maiden May" (before 1882), "stands at 'Why?' " Life as a dialectic process she comes to accept, but in back of the process there yet "lies an unsolved mystery."

After Mrs. Rossetti died in 1886, Christina was more alone than ever. In the years remaining before her own death in 1894, she occupied herself almost entirely with devotional writing. Though this writing, the poetry as well as the prose, is not without imaginative qualities, much of it tends to be dutiful articulation of Christian doctrines, of biblical attitudes and sentiments. For Christina, the great battle between the flesh and the spirit seemed over; or, if not over, there was no longer a head-on clash with traumatic emotional discord. Her own will she now could more easily submit to the will of God. And yet, when confined to bed in her final illness, apparently in one last effort to convince herself and to bolster her courage, she had placed so that she could see it at all times the following text from Isaiah (12:2): "I will trust, and not be afraid."[20] That her heart and soul were never truly at rest is perhaps best attested to by her last-written poem:

> Sleeping at last, the trouble and tumult over,
>   Sleeping at last, the struggle and horror
>   past,
> Cold and white, out of sight of friend and of
>   lover,
>   Sleeping at last.
>
> No more a tired heart downcast or overcast,
>   No more pangs that wring or shifting fears
>   that hover,
> Sleeping at last in a dreamless sleep locked
>   fast.
>
> Fast asleep. Singing birds in their leafy cover
>   Cannot wake her, nor shake her the gusty blast,
> Under the purple thyme and the purple clover
>   Sleeping at last.

(417)

These lines, says William Michael, "form a very fitting close to her poetic performance, the longing for rest . . . being most marked throughout the whole course of her writings."[21] No reader of the canon of Christina's poetry disagrees with his observation.

CHAPTER 5

"Monna Innominata" and *"Later Life"*

IN 1881, *A Pageant and Other Poems* was published. The title poem, "The Months: A Pageant," consists of a succession of twelve animated scenes appropriate for each month of the year; and these scenes are artfully linked by personified figures. Intended for dramatic presentation by children, "The Months" can also be enjoyed by adults. Mackenzie Bell points out that the poem "holds a unique place among Christina's long poems; it is cheerful throughout, with not a single note reminding the reader of sorrow."[1] In addition to "The Months," the *Pageant* volume contains a few noteworthy ballads and lyrics; but the important poems are in the sonnet form, one of Christina's favorite poetic modes. She first became adept in using the form in the summer of 1848, when she and her brothers engaged in *boutes-rimés*, a game of composing verses to a given set of rhymes.

By the end of the year, the sonnet was common among her serious poems; and she thereafter turned to it frequently to express almost any theme in her secular and religious verse. Love, however, is the central theme of the two sonnet sequences in *A Pageant and Other Poems*, "Monna Innominata" and "Later Life." Individual sonnets in "Monna Innominata" develop motifs that are found in many of the secular love poems. Indeed, the sequence as a whole captures the quintessence of some of her best nondevotional poetry. On the other hand, individual sonnets in "Later Life" develop motifs of religious beliefs that are representative of those in her devotional poetry. In these sonnets, as in many of the devotional poems, the beliefs are, for the most part, expressed didactically. As a sequence, "Later Life" is loosely structured, and it lacks the emotional depth of "Monna Innominata." Of the two sequences, "Monna Innominata" is obviously superior, and contemporary reviewers singled it out for special praise.

I   *"Monna Innominata"*

"Monna Innominata" consists of fourteen sonnets, written over the years from 1866 to 1881 (most of them closer to the earlier date), and a prose prefatory note. This note, William Michael asserted, was a "blind interposed to draw off attention from the writer in her proper person."[2] Actually, the note functions not so much as a device to disguise Christina's identity as to explain the point of view from which the sonnets are written. Alluding to Dante and Petrarch, she says that the celebrated ladies of their sonnets, although not without charm, are "scant of attractiveness." Many other "unnamed ladies," though perhaps possessing "poetic aptitude," did not express their feelings. In brief the point of view of Dante's and Petrarch's sonnets, indeed of most love sonnets, is that of the lover. Elizabeth B. Browning is an exception, but her song is joyous, Christina observes. Had she been "unhappy," she might have been immortalized as "an inimitable 'donna innominata.'"

What Christina clearly proposed for herself was a sonnet sequence on the theme of unfulfilled love and therefore sad in mood, but of a love idealized. The love in "Monna Innominata" is similar in certain respects to the platonic love expressed by Dante for Beatrice, but it is significantly different because it is poetically expressed from the lady's point of view. As William Michael also observed, the sequence is a "personal utterance — an intensely personal one."[3] As with his claim that the prose note was a blind, this point likewise appears too strongly pressed. In any case, his comment is not very enlightening, for almost all of Christina's secular poetry is "intensely personal" in the sense that she was, as already noted, an extremely self-conscious person who subjectified severely before articulating her emotions. That William's remark is intended to direct consideration to Charles Bagot Cayley, a close friend whose marriage proposal she declined in 1866, as the subject of the sonnets seems likely. Be that as it may, the personal subject is less important than the treatment of the theme.

"Monna Innominata" is a dialectic on the desire for earthly love versus the advisability of postponing that love in hopes of its spiritual realization in heaven. Though in each sonnet the speaker professes her love, most of the sonnets present mental and emotional states of the speaker contingent upon love's being unfulfilled. The key background factor of the sequence, emphatically presented in the first sonnet, is the separation of the speaker from the one she loves. This separation produces an ambivalence, which characterizes the sequence as a whole. In Sonnet 1, the ambivalence is given its simplest form: separation, painful though it is, is to be preferred because the happiness of meeting again would only mean greater sorrow at parting. By Sonnet 3, the ambivalence is expressed in realistic-idealistic terms: realistic because of her awareness that "only in a dream we are at one"; idealistic because of her preference for the dream rather than the real experience. Before the sequence has developed very far, the speaker has committed herself, not to striving to actualize the love experience, but to postponing, idealizing, and spiritualizing it.

Sonnet 4 deals with the immeasurability of love and prepares in a general way for the consideration of love as spiritual. The next sonnet acknowledges her subservience and her avowal to love "without stint"; but, more importantly in Sonnet 5, she commends her lover to God and urges him to dedicate his life to Him, thus introducing into the relationship a new consideration, the primacy of the love of God. This primacy is the theme of Sonnet 6: "I love, as you would have me, God the most; / Would lose not Him, but you must not be lost." But the decision to place divine love above human love, perhaps easy enough to consider, is not easy to live by. There persists the desire for earthly love at the same time that the speaker dedicates herself to the love of God. The disturbing question is whether anyone can commit oneself fully to both human and divine love.

With the priority for the speaker established, she then (in a mildly argumentative tone and style that bring Donne to mind but without his verve) considers mental and emotional states resulting from having made such a decision. By Sonnet 13, all of the tensions appear resolved; she reaffirms her faith that the future is in God's hands and again commends her lover to God. At first, Sonnet 13 seems to be the climax of the sequence; but Sonnet 14, with its plaintive cry of unfulfilled love, redirects the theme, shifts the tone, and climaxes the sequence:

> Youth gone, and beauty gone if ever there
> Dwelt beauty in so poor a face as this;
> Youth gone and beauty, what remains of
>   bliss?
> I will not bind fresh roses in my hair.
> To shame a cheek at best but little fair, —

> Leave youth his roses, who can bear a
>   thorn, —
> I will not seek for blossoms anywhere,
> Except such common flowers as blow with
>   corn.
> Youth gone and beauty gone, what doth
>   remain?
> The longing of a heart pent up forlorn,
> A silent heart whose silence loves and
>   longs;
> The silence of a heart which sang its songs
> While youth and beauty made a summer morn,
> Silence of love that cannot sing again.
>
>   (63–64)

This sonnet has a great impact because the reader has just been lulled by the preceding sonnet into believing that the speaker has attained a happy resolution to the separation dilemma and to the problem of human versus divine love only to learn in Sonnet 14 that her regrets are more deeply felt than ever. The closing line, "Silence of love that cannot sing again," poignantly catches the disappointment that could not be suppressed.

II *"Later Life"*

"Later Life" consists of twenty-eight sonnets. Twenty-four are addressed to listeners who are regarded as friends and fellow-sinners. Four (3, 4, 5, 8) are addressed to God and beseech Him to remember the struggling Christian and to give him the power to love. The element that unifies all of the sonnets in the sequence is the speaker's exhortation to her listeners to persevere in their efforts to love God and in their hope for redemption.

In the first fifteen sonnets, the speaker's voice is fairly confident about accepting the trials of this life while looking forward to salvation. But in Sonnet 16, a slight change in tone prepares for the personal outburst that comes in Sonnet 17:

> I am sick of where I am and where I am not,
> I am sick of foresight and of memory,
> I am sick of all that I have and all I see,
> I am sick of self. . . .
>
>   (78)

This sonnet is pivotal, for it changes the thematic development of the sequence. This one sonnet, with considerable force, shatters the optimism of the speaker. With Sonnet 18, her recovery begins, and the rest of the sequence is concerned with rebuilding a weakened faith.

As Christina often does in her poetry, she turns to the cycle of nature for a parallel to that of life. Autumn-winter-spring-summer, the pattern of death and rebirth, of sadness and joy, is traced in Sonnets 18–23. In Sonnets 21 and 22, her spirit gains strength by recalling her delight in scenes of nature while on a Switzerland-Italy trip. In Sonnet 23, the application to man's condition of the lesson learned from nature is presented:

> This dead and living world befits our case
>   Who live and die: we live in wearied hope,
> We die in hope not dead.
>
> (80)

Sonnet 24 stresses the central problem of the sequence: a person "hankers after Heaven, but clings to earth." The sonnet implores the listeners to reorient their thinking. The things of the world must be rejected, and people must set their sights on heaven. The reorientation continues in Sonnets 25 and 26, with special emphasis in Sonnet 26 on the vanity of everything: "This Life we live is dead for all its breath." One should, therefore, look forward without regret to death, which is personified and addressed in the last line: "O Death who art not Death."

The next stage (Sonnet 27) in the argument moves from the acknowledgment of death as entry into spiritual life to speculation on what death will actually be like. Finally, with death approaching, the speaker fears that she herself "May miss the goal at last."[4] The fear is not directly allayed in Sonnet 28, the last one, because the motif is shifted; and the sequence concludes with the statement that the "unforgotten dearest dead" are waiting for one, "brimful of knowledge" and "brimful of love for you and love for me." The sonnet expresses belief in immortality, but any reference to whether or not the speaker herself expects to reach that goal is carefully avoided.

The sonnets in both sequences are similar in technique to Christina's other sonnets. They are Petrarchan, conforming loosely to the traditional octave and sestet division, with the sestet more often complementary than antithetical to the octave. Only occasionally does Christina use enjambment in moving from the octave to the sestet. Though she retains the two major rhetorical divisions, she takes considerable freedom with the rhyme scheme throughout. The *abba abba* pattern in the octave is most common, but she varies this pattern fairly frequently, particularly in the second quatrain. The pattern in the sestet varies greatly, though she does limit herself to three different rhymes. Sight and approximate rhymes abound, but the reader often regards them as annoying infelicities.

Christina's sonnets differ from her brother Dante's because they lack his concentrated imagery, intensity, elaborateness, richness, and, in general, his power. But his practice did influence her, and his philosophy of sonnet composition, as stated by him in a letter to Hall Caine, is one to which she would have subscribed:

Sonnets of mine *could not appear* in any book which contained . . . rigid rules as to rhyme. . . . I neither follow them, nor agree with them as regards the English language. Every sonnet-writer should show full capability of conforming to them in *many* instances, but never to deviate from them in English must pinion both thought and diction, and, (mastery once proved) a series gains rather than loses by such varieties as do not lessen the only *absolute* aim — that of beauty. The English sonnet *too much* tampered with becomes a sort of bastard madrigal. *Too much, invariably* restricted, it degenerates into a Shibboleth.[5]

CHAPTER 6

Devotional Poems

B Y general agreement, Christina Rossetti must be ranked among great religious poets in English such as John Donne, George Herbert and Henry Vaughan of the seventeenth century and John Keble, John Henry Newman, Coventry Patmore, and Gerard Manley Hopkins of the nineteenth. Her religious poems constitute the largest single group in her canon. Four hundred-fifty of them are found under the heading "Devotional Poems," in *The Poetical Works,* but many other poems not included under this heading are religious in tone, or at least spiritual in inspiration, though they are less doctrinal in content. In fact, in some poems the religious and secular elements are so naturally blended that labeling the poems as either religious or secular is impossible.

Three hundred thirty-two of the devotional poems are arranged under eight subheadings: (1) "Songs for Strangers and Pilgrims"; (2) "Some Feasts and Fasts"; (3) "Divers Worlds: Time and Eternity"; (4) "New Jerusalem and its Citizens"; (5) "Christ Our All in All"; (6) "Out of the Deep Have I Called Unto Thee, O Lord"; (7) "Gifts and Graces"; (8) "The World: Self-Destruction." The poems under these subheadings appeared in *Verses* (1893), a republication by the Society for Promoting Christian Knowledge of poems from three earlier prose-poetry volumes: *Called to be Saints* (1881), *Time Flies* (1885), and *The Face of the Deep* (1892). The subheadings also derive from *Verses,* but William Michael changed their order in *The Poetical Works.* The remaining 118 devotional poems are not given any special classification.

In the traditional Christian way, Christina thought of her life as a pilgrimage. Not surprisingly, therefore, the devotional poems, viewed as a whole, depict the pilgrimage of a soul to heaven. Within that framework, two underlying themes unify the poems: the hope

76

of salvation, and the expectation of fulfilling this hope through devotion to Jesus Christ as redeemer. Individual poems present biblical precepts that can guide the pilgrim on his journey; and, if he lives by these precepts, the heart's restlessness will be quieted in this life at the same time that the soul is being prepared for the next.

Since the Bible and other religious writings are the main source for Christina's aspirations and consolations, many of the images and sentiments in the devotional poems tend to be conventional or ready-made ones. But such is less the case with the poems that comprise the smaller, nonclassified group, especially those written during the 1850s and 1860s. In these, the personal tone is stronger; and the emotions are more intense.

I *Early Religious Poems*

The theme common to many of the early religious poems has three stages: the vanity of all earthly things, the anticipation of an early death, and the looking forward to heaven. (This theme is also common in the nondevotional poems, but often without or with less optimism about attaining heaven.) In developing the theme, Christina frequently draws special attention to the natural world and its beauty; but, as she says in "Sweet Death," why care about the passing away of beauty in the world or even about our own death when after death comes life with God?

Some of the poems capture Christina's most devout and prayerful moments. These poems become devotional shrines where, in the words of a contemporary reviewer, "we find her on her knees, with a strong faith, a deep sense of spiritual needs, a feeling of the real littleness of the life passing around us, of the true greatness of what is to come after, a sense of the presence of the living God before whom she bows down her soul into the dust; and here she is another woman. As she sinks her poetry rises, and gushes up out of her heart to heaven in strains sad, sweet, tender, and musical that a saint might envy."[1] "The Three Enemies" (1851) and "Good Friday" (1862) are such "shrines." Both are meditations upon the passion of Christ, and the speaker humbly implores Christ's intercession on her behalf in gaining salvation.

In poem after poem, the speaker's mind dwells on thoughts of heaven. Her main concern is with the spiritual peace and joy that will be found there, but she also depicts heaven as a place that will delight the senses. In "Paradise" (1854), for example, recalling Genesis and Revelation, she describes her dream of heaven: the fair

flowers, the singing birds, the music of the fourfold river, the sweet
fruit of the tree of life; she sees, too,

> the golden streets begin,
> And outskirts of the glassy pool.
> Oh harps, oh crowns of plenteous stars,
> Oh green palm branches many-leaved. . . .
>
> (181)

Christina's belief was in the literal existence of a heaven, and she
tells us:

> I hope to see these things again
> But not as once in dreams by night;
> To see them with my very sight,
> And touch and handle and attain. . . .
>
> (181)

One characteristic of the religious poems of the early 1850s is the
view that, though the poet-speaker feels undeserving, her confidence in obtaining God's love and in achieving salvation is fairly
strong. By about 1857, however, the feeling of unworthiness begins
to dominate more and more poems. In "I Will Lift Up Mine Eyes
Unto the Hills" (1856), which evinces the same trust in God as the
singer of Psalm 121, her soul "beats her wings / And pants to fly
away / Up to immortal things / In the heavenly day"; but, in "A
Better Resurrection" (1857), she cannot envision the everlasting
hills: "I lift mine eyes, but dimmed with grief / No everlasting hills I
see." The dejection in "A Better Resurrection" is even stronger in
"Introspective," the nonreligious poem written on the same day.

As in Christina's secular poetry, so too in the religious, her moods
can change suddenly.[2] Her typical mood, however, is described by
Paul Elmer More as "a passive surrender to the powers of life, a
religious acquiescence, which wavers between a plaintive pathos and
a sublime exultation of faith."[3] Pehaps the poem that best ex-
emplifies this mood is "Passing Away," which was written not long
after Christina reached her thirtieth birthday in December, 1860,
and about which William Michael observed that "her thoughts as to
the transit of years may have been more than ordinarily solemn." He
added that he always regarded the poem "as the very summit and
mountain-top of Christina's work."[4] Swinburne, having read the

poem, exclaimed, "By God! that's one of the finest things ever written!"[5]; and later readers have concurred with his verdict. The poem deserves to be cited in full.

> Passing away, saith the World, passing
>   away:
> Chances, beauty, and youth, sapped day
>   by day:
> Thy life never continueth in one stay.
> Is the eye waxen dim, is the dark hair
>   changing to grey
> That hath won neither laurel nor bay?
> I shall clothe myself in Spring and bud
>   in May:
> Thou, root-stricken, shalt not rebuild
>   thy decay
> On my bosom for aye.
> Then I answered: Yea.
>
> Passing away, saith my Soul, passing away:
> With its burden of fear and hope, of
>   labour and play,
> Hearken what the past doth witness and
>   say:
> Rust in thy gold, a moth is in thine
>   array,
> A canker is in thy bud, thy leaf must
>   decay.
> At midnight, at cockcrow, at morning,
>   one certain day
> Lo the Bridegroom shall come and shall
>   not delay;
> Watch thou and pray.
> Then I answered: Yea.
>
> Passing away, saith my God, passing away:
> Winter passeth after the long delay:
> New grapes on the vine, new figs on the
>   tender spray,
> Turtle calleth turtle in Heaven's May.
> Though I tarry, wait for Me, trust Me,
>   watch and pray:
> Arise, come away, night is past and lo
>   it is day,

My love, My sister, My spouse, thou shalt
   hear Me say.
Then I answered: Yea.

                                    (191)

Taking ideas and images from 1 John, Matthew, James, Mark, and
particularly in the last stanza from the Song of Solomon (2),
Christina applies them to her own situation in life and develops a
poem that is, though dramatically structured, an intensely personal
utterance. In More's analysis of the poem, he writes: "Even her
monotone, which after long continuation becomes monotony, affects
one here as a subtle device heightening the note of subdued fervour
and religious resignation; the repetition of the rhyming vowel
creates the feeling of a secret expectancy cherished through the
weariness of a frustrate life."[6] Packer, too, in praising the poem, calls
attention to the effective fusion of the technical elements: "What is
noteworthy . . . is that the rhythm, diction, and word-order express
the thought and emotion so naturally and with such inevitable
rightness that one scarcely observes the technical triumph of mono-
rhyme sustained throughout."[7]

From 1861–65 (but especially in 1864), the self-reproach in-
creases; and at times she expresses doubts of her love of God. The
pleading becomes more insistent, and touches of near-despair appear more frequently. Some of the poems in this period which depict
a deep sense of unworthiness are "Out of the Deep" (1862), "For a
Mercy Received" (1863), "The Lowest Place" (1863), "Come Unto
Me" (1864), "Who Shall Deliver Me?" (1864), "Despised and Rejected" (1864), and "I Know You Not" (c. 1864). As most of the titles
indicate, Christina again relied for poetic inspiration on biblical passages dealing with spiritual conditions closely paralleling her own.
In turning to these passages, she must have obtained comfort from
the realization that her feelings were not unique and from the hope
that is held out for the self-deprecating individual.

The best known of the poems in this group is "The Lowest Place":

Give me the lowest place; not that I dare
   Ask for that lowest place, but Thou hast died
That I might live and share
   Thy glory by Thy side.

Give me the lowest place: or if for me
   That lowest place too high, make one more low

> Where I may sit and see
> My God and love Thee so.
>
> (237)

Simply and explicitly the poem renders in personal terms the parable of the wedding guest from Luke (14: 7–11) and its lesson: "For whosoever exalteth himself shall be abased; and he that humbleth himself shall be exalted." Of special note is Christina's use of phonetic recurrence (initial, internal, and end) to establish the rhythmical sound pattern. "As an expression of her permanent attitude of mind in the region of faith and hope," wrote William Michael, "Christina evidently laid some stress on this little poem."[8] The last stanza was inscribed on her tombstone in Highgate Cemetery.

How severe Christina's internal struggle could be is indicated in "Who Shall Deliver Me?":

> God strengthen me to bear myself;
> That heaviest weight of all to bear,
> Inalienable weight of care.
>
> All others are outside myself;
> I lock my door and bar them out,
> The turmoil, tedium, gad-about.
>
> I lock my door upon myself,
> And bar them out; but who shall wall
> Self from myself, most loathed of all?
>
> . . . .
>
> God harden me against myself,
> This coward with pathetic voice
> Who craves for ease, and rest, and joys:
>
> Myself, arch-traitor to myself;
> My hollowest friend, my deadliest foe,
> My clog whatever road I go.
>
> (238)

Christina saw her own dilemma of the divided self in terms of Romans 7:19: "For the good that I would, I do not: but the evil which I would not, that I do." The difficulty of acting according to the law, which is spiritual, at the same time that one suppresses natural desires is the crux of the dilemma that weighed sorely on Christina's conscience.

Packer cites in conjunction with her reading of "Who Shall Deliver Me?" an entry from *Time Flies*, Christina's published diary.[9] The entry records an incident Christina calls a "Parable of Nature" and concerns a spider and its shadow:

They jerked, zigzagged, advanced, retreated, he and his shadow posturing in ungainly indissoluble harmony. He seemed exasperated, fascinated, desperately endeavouring and utterly hopeless.

What could it mean? One meaning and one only suggested itself. That spider saw without recognising his black double, and was mad to disengage himself from the horrible pursuing inalienable presence. . . .

To me this self-haunted spider appears a figure of each obstinate impenitent sinner, who having outlived enjoyment remains isolated irretrievably with his own horrible loathsome self.[10]

This passage and "Who Shall Deliver Me?" must be interpreted in relation to Christina's "sister" poems and other secular poems of the 1860s dealing with the fragmented ego and with attempts to integrate the personality.

"Despised and Rejected" in a sense is an even more disconsolate poem than "Who Shall Deliver Me?". Like the servant of Isaiah 52 and 53, the prophesied Christ was denied entrance into the house (and heart) of the speaker. All night Christ pleaded to be let in:

> So till the break of day:
> Then died away
> That voice, in silence as of sorrow;
> Then footsteps echoing like a sigh
> Passed me by,
> Lingering footsteps slow to pass.
> On the morrow
> I saw upon the grass
> Each footprint marked in blood, and
>   on my door
> The mark of blood for evermore.

(241–42)

The fear of actually rejecting Christ and of being unworthy of his grace are fears associated with Christina's lifelong fear of not being among those chosen for salvation on the day of judgment. "I Know

You Not," a title suggested by Matthew 7:23, expresses this fear of those who do not heed the call of Christ: "He called, but they refused to know; / So now He hears their cry no more" (244).

After 1865 the self-reproach eases, and less anguish and desperation are found in the devotional poems. By the mid-1870s, Christina is already engaged in writing the religious prose and verse intended for the edification of readers and published by the Society for Promoting Christian Knowledge. By the late 1880s, she has practically become a religious recluse, as she acknowledged in a letter in 1887 to her sister-in-law Lucy, the wife of William Michael. "I now live," she wrote, "so much in the other world — or at least I ought to do so, having my chief Treasure there."[11]

The Society for Promoting Christian Knowledge publications express, with some exceptions, a conditioned acceptance of Christian doctrines and an objectifying, to a degree, of religious experience. While Christina is still speaking for herself, she also serves as spokesman for the Church. The voice that once held converse with her soul and strove to speak with God now addresses her fellow pilgrims, guiding, consoling, and urging them onward. Poetically rendered, this voice has power to uplift the spirit of the Christian and to encourage him to turn his eyes toward heaven. But she cannot always suppress her innermost feelings; and, when these come forth, they charge the poems with an intensity to which the reader responds. Some of these more personal poems, though they are not characteristic of the Society for Promoting Christian Knowledge poems, are therefore singled out for comment in the following discussion.

II *"Songs for Strangers and Pilgrims"*

Most of the poems in "Songs for Strangers and Pilgrims" are rather formal in style and rely heavily upon rhetorical statement for their effect. The main message of the section is that fellow Christians should have patience, for Almighty love will prevail in time:

> Watch till the day
> When all save only Love shall pass away.
> Then Love rejoicing shall forget to weep,
> Shall hope or fear no more, or watch or
>   sleep,
> But only love and stint not, deep beyond
>   deep.

> Now we sow love in tears, but then shall
>   reap.
> Have patience as True Love's own flock
>   of sheep:
> Have patience with His Love
> Who served for us, Who reigns for us
>   above.
>
> (121–22)

Other related themes exhort readers to give themselves to prayer, to take up their own crosses and follow Christ, and to submit their wills to the will of God.

The didacticism becomes somewhat heavy in some of the longer poems; but poems occasionally, though still didactic, utilize short lines and spare imagery to produce a lighter impression. For modern readers, these poems are probably more enjoyable than most others in this section. One such is "Joy Is But Sorrow":

> Joy is but sorrow,
> While we know
> It ends to-morrow: —
> Even so!
> Joy with lifted veil
> Shows a face as pale
> As the fair changing moon so
>   fair and frail.
>
> Pain is but pleasure,
> If we know
> It heaps up treasure: —
> Even so!
> Turn, transfigured Pain,
> Sweetheart, turn again,
> For fair thou art as moonrise
>   after rain.
>
> (125)

III *"Some Feasts and Fasts"*

"Some Feasts and Fasts" is an abbreviated version of John Keble's *The Christian Year* (1827), a book of hymns and religious poetry that remained popular throughout the century. Christina's copy contains marginal notes and personal illustrations; and, like Keble's, Christina's arrangement follows the liturgical calendar, with most of the poems intended for special observances in connection with the two great feasts: Christmas and Easter. Additional poems commemorate some of the major saints of the Anglican Church. Because Christina's pattern of worship coincided closely with the liturgy of her Church, these poems that cover the ecclesiastical year illustrate the range of her orthodox religious devotions.

The poems begin appropriately with Advent and speak of the need for, and the expectation of, the coming of a merciful Christ. In "Christmas Day," Christina celebrates the birth of the Christ-child while already looking forward, as is traditional, to the passion and crucifixion, the culmination of Christ's redemptive mission on earth:

> . . . .
> And Flower of Babies was their King,
> Jesus Christ our Lord:
> Lily of lilies He
> Upon His Mother's knee;
> Rose of roses, soon to be
> Crowned with thorns on leaf-
> less tree.
>
> (158)

"Christmas Day" has that unsophisticated, childlike candor usually associated with a saintly person's easy acceptance of the gospel story of Christmas. This *ingenu* quality is found also in Christina's Christmas carols.

Christmas celebrates the central doctrine of Christianity, the incarnation, an act of God which manifests his great love for man but which also calls upon man to demonstrate his love for God. It is understandable, therefore, that love should be one of the principal themes of Christina's devotional poetry and particularly of those poems written for the Feast of Christmas. "Christmastide" is one of these:

> Love came down at Christmas,
> Love all lovely, Love Divine;
> Love was born at Christmas,
> Star and Angels gave the sign.
>
> Worship we the Godhead,
> Love Incarnate, Love Divine;
> Worship we our Jesus:
> But wherewith for sacred sign?

Love shall be our token,
    Love be yours and love be mine,
Love to God and all men,
    Love for plea and gift and sign.

(159)

In poems for the Lenten season, the emphasis shifts to man's sinful nature and to his need to beseech God's mercy. "Ash Wednesday," a keynote poem for the opening of Lent, simply and forcefully presents the penitential and merciful aspects of Eastertide:

My God, my God, have mercy on my sin,
For it is great; and if I should begin
To tell it all, the day would be too
    small
To tell it in.

My God, Thou wilt have mercy on my sin
For Thy Love's sake: yea, if I should
    begin
To tell This all, the day would be too
    small
To tell it in.

(163)

The poems following Easter celebrate other important holydays, vigils, and feasts of saints in the church year.

IV *"Divers Worlds: Time and Eternity"*

The poems in "Divers Worlds: Time and Eternity" contrast, as the title indicates, earth and heaven, and the concepts of time and eternity. Earth is "This near-at-hand land [that] breeds pain by measure"; heaven, "That far-away land [that] overflows with treasure." On earth, "Time passeth away"; but, in heaven, "Eternity cometh to stay." Most of the descriptions of heaven are general and conventional, in terms such as these: "Far, far away lies the beautiful land" (196) and

We know not when, we know not where,
    We know not what that world will be;
But this we know — it will be fair
    To see.

(196)

But, as usual, when Christina's thoughts dwell on paradise, concrete details from biblical passages are also recalled: "There are gems and gold and inlets pearled; / There the verdure fadeth not again; / There no clinging tendrils droop uncurled" (197). Fuller descriptions of heaven and its glories are found in "New Jerusalem and Its Citizens." In this section, "Divers Worlds: Time and Eternity," one of the shortest poems is also one of the best:

> Heaven is not far, tho' far the sky
>   Overarching earth and main.
> It takes not long to live and die,
>   Die, revive, and rise again.
> Not long: how long? Oh long re-echoing song!
>   O Lord, how long?

                                                              (193–94)

Of this poem Oliver Elton says: "the master-mood of two-thirds of her musings is heard in one short flight of six lines."[12]

V   *"New Jerusalem and Its Citizens"*

Christina's inspiration for most of the poems in "New Jerusalem and Its Citizens" comes from apocalyptic passages in the Old and New Testaments but especially from The Revelation of Saint John the Divine. New Jerusalem is "built of gold / Of crystal, pearl and gem," a city "where song nor gem / Nor fruit nor waters cease." Its citizens, robed in white and with palm-branch in hand, spend their time worshipping the enthroned God face to face. The way to gain the Holy City is through imitation of the lives of the saints:

> I think of the saints I have known,
>   and lift up mine eyes
> To the far-away home of beautiful
>   Paradise,
> Where the song of saints gives voice
>   to an undividing sea
> On whose plain their feet stand firm
>   while they keep their jubilee.

                                                              (213)

Through love, through obedience to the divine will, and through patience, one will be able to join the heavenly chorus of "happy hearts ... chanting psalms, / Endless Te Deum for the ended fight." As in the Bible, so in these poems is expressed the belief in the actual existence of the New Jerusalem for the redeemed after the Resurrection of the dead at the Last Judgment.

VI   *"Christ Our All in All"*

Many of the poems in "Christ Our All in All" are monologue prayers addressed to Christ, but others are dialogues. The speaker acknowledges her unworthiness of salvation; but she is then reassured that, however unworthy she may seem in her own eyes, she will be saved if she gives herself humbly and wholly to Christ. In "Lord God of Hosts, most Holy and most High," the speaker asks a series of questions about the means to salvation. Each stanza ends with Christ's answer: "My love of thee." This refrain echoes as a motif through almost all of the poems in this section. Christ as king of kings is adored; and, as in John 10, he is regarded as "Shepherd and Door, our Life and Truth and Way." Most of these poems, like most of Christina's other devotional poems, are written in an eight- or ten-syllable line. Usually, however, Christina's most effective line is the shorter six-syllable line with an occasional four, as in this Blakean example:

> 'Little Lamb, who lost thee?' —
>   'I myself, none other.' —
> 'Little Lamb, who found thee?' —
>   'Jesus, Shepherd, Brother.
> Ah, Lord, what I cost Thee!
>   Canst Thou still desire?' —
> 'Still Mine arms surround thee,
>   Still I lift thee higher,
> Draw thee nigher.'

(223)

VII   *"Out of the Deep Have I Called unto Thee, O Lord"*

In the poems in "Out of the Deep Have I Called unto Thee, O Lord" (Psalm 130), the speaker cries out to the Lord, imploring his love for one "ashamed to seek Thy Face / As tho' I loved Thee as Thy saints love Thee." The speaker, considering herself unworthy, begs: "Lord, drop . . . / One Drop from Thine own Heart, and overweigh / My guilt, my folly, even my heart of stone." In these poems the anguish of a sinner is heard again and again along with a brief prayer based on Psalm 42:

> The longing of my heart cries out
>   to Thee
> The hungering thirsting longing
>   of my heart. . . .

> (269)

Like all religious poets, Christina of course was aware of the fundamental paradoxes in Christianity: one must die in order to gain eternal life, God becomes man in the incarnation, Christ is crucified but wins redemption for man. As did Donne, Herbert, and other religious writers before her, Christina often uses paradoxes of Christian teaching to achieve rhetorical and structural tension. Such is the case with a number of poems in this section, and one example is "It is not death, O Christ, to die for Thee." In it, the opening paradox is followed by another: "that silence of a silent land / Which speaks Thy praise." Next comes the paradox of the "Darkness of death" making "Thy dear lovers see." These paradoxes culminate in the final paradox from Revelation 1:4: that Christ was, is, and will be. The poet then returns to the paradoxical theme of the poem: "Death is not death."

Other paradoxes appear in this section: "Lord, I believe, help Thou my unbelief"; "O Lord, on Whom we gaze and dare not gaze"; "O Lord God, hear the silence of each soul"; "O Christ our Light, Whom even in darkness we (So we look up) discern and gaze upon." In fact, Christina plays with the sounds and meanings of words more deliberately than usual in many of these poems. In some instances, the effect is forceful, as for example in these lines: "Unsnared, unscared by world or flesh or devil," and "disgrace me not with uttermost disgrace; / But pour on me ungracious, pour Thy grace." In other instances, the punning strikes one as too artificial and ostentatiously clever, as in these examples: ". . . That we may mount aspiring, and aspire / Still while we mount," and "My price Thy priceless Blood; and therefore I / Price of Thy priceless Blood. . . ."

VIII *"Gifts and Graces"*

The poems in the section "Gifts and Graces" again stress the means by which a pilgrim reaches the New Jerusalem. Among these are fear, faith, hope, patience, prudence, obedience, humility, wisdom, and — above all — love. In poem after poem, the speaker asks for the grace from God to love Him and to do His will, for it is by love that man gains heaven:

> . . . love lifts up a face like any rose
> Flushing and sweet above a thorny stem,
> Softly protesting that the way he knows;
> And as for faith and hope, will carry them
> Safe to the gate of New Jerusalem,
> Where light shines full and where the
>   palm-tree blows.

(273)

IX *"The World: Self-Destruction"*

The poems in "The World: Self-Destruction" are intended as a grave warning to the sinner. In most other devotional poems, the Christian possesses a sensitive appreciation of temporal pleasures and beauties, but he is cautioned not to become too preoccupied with these. For the sinner, however, the world is seen as "mouldy, worm-eaten, grey," as

> . . . nauseous sweet
> Puffed up and perishing;
> A hollow thing,
> A lie, a vanity
> Tinsel and paint.

(283)

In such a world, bereft of God's graces, the sinner can only despair; for his life contrasts sharply with that of the Christian pilgrim who, though falling short of being saintly, nonetheless strives to emulate the saints and has reason therefore to be hopeful of salvation.

CHAPTER 7

Children's Verse: Sing-Song

WHEN *Sing-Song: A Nursery Rhyme Book* appeared in late 1872 after Christina had many difficulties in settling on a publisher and illustrator, reviewers and the general reader praised the poems and the 120 illustrations by Arthur Hughes. The work is historically important, for it contained traditional didactic mode poems as well as nondidactic ones that reflected the new trend in nineteenth-century children's literature. Like most writers of children's verse, Christina is indebted to "Mother Goose" collections not only for inspiration but for subject matter and particular types of verse. Relatively few poems in *Sing-Song*, however, exhibit to the same degree the fanciful qualities and the catchy musical strains of "Mother Goose." Indeed, though the subtitle, "A Nursery Rhyme Book," suggests a collection of rhymes for nursery-aged children, many of the poems are not, strictly considered, rhymes; and they frequently are directed to older children and even to adults who would be expected to interpret them to young listeners. In these poems, the reader is conscious of the prevailing adult point of view and of the hand of an accomplished poet who is controlling the subtle melody and the thematic development.

The "Mother Goose" type instructional rhymes in *Sing-Song* are intended to make it easy and pleasant for young children to learn addition, time measurement, money denominations, the seasons, and the colors. (Christina also wrote an alphabet rhyme but it was not included in *Sing-Song*). These poems are rather pedestrian, except one of the color rhymes. After a series of questions and answers, beginning with "What is pink? a rose is pink / By the foundation's brink," the poem concludes with the ejaculatory couplet: "What is orange? why, an orange, / Just an orange!" Other instructional rhymes that are of the riddle variety inform the readers that "needles have eyes, but they cannot see," that "a pin has a head, but has no hair," or

that "a captain's log is not a log." Though the language of these
rhymes is at times a little formal, the tones tend to be fairly light.
Some, however, are philosophically serious, as in this example which
is obviously aimed at adult readers:

> What are heavy? sea-sand and sorrow:
> What are brief? to-day and tomorrow:
> What are frail? Spring blossoms and
>   youth:
> What are deep? the ocean and truth.

(430)

The world of Mother Goose is inhabited by all kinds of people that
children find interesting: the odd ones who fascinate them, and the
normal ones who do ordinary things but who sometimes act unpredictably. In the world of *Sing-Song*, the people manifest few unusual traits. There are babies, mothers, fathers, sisters, brothers,
wives, husbands, milkmaids, a sailor, and a postman who do what is
customary; but the poems about babies are the most common. Some
are enjoyable verses such as the following two:

> Angels at the foot,
>   And Angels at the head,
> And like a curly little lamb
>   My pretty babe in bed.

(426)

> Baby cry —
>   Oh fie! —
> At the physic in the cup:
>   Gulp it twice
> And gulp it thrice,
>   Baby gulp it up.

(426)

Many of the "baby" poems echo the stock themes and sentiments of
the children's poetry of the period, as for example this poem which is
designed to elicit sympathy for an orphan child:

> My baby has a father and a mother,
>   Rich little baby!

>   Fatherless, motherless, I know another
>   Forlorn as may be:
>   Poor Little baby!

>   (426)

Despite the sentimental nature of the themes in the "baby" poems, as in other poems, Christina often avoids being maudlin by using terse statement and simple diction and syntax, as seen in these verses:

>   Love me, — I love you,
>   Love me, my baby;
>   Sing it high, sing it low,
>   Sing it as may be.

>   Mother's arms under you,
>   Her eyes above you;
>   Sing it high, sing it low,
>   Love me, — I love you.

>   (426)

Though lullabies are probably the earliest form of nursery rhymes, they have traditionally exhibited great skill in composition. It may be that the ordinary singer of rhymes as well as the professional poet finds a special and appealing challenge in adapting technical elements of verse to the slumber-inducing purpose of lullabies. At any rate, Christina wrote several, and one of them is the most musical poem in *Sing-Song:*

>   Lullaby, oh lullaby!
>   Flowers are closed and lambs are sleeping;
>   Lullaby, oh lullaby!
>   Stars are up, the moon is peeping;
>   Lullaby, oh lullaby!
>   While the birds are silence keeping,
>   (Lullaby, oh lullaby!)
>   Sleep, my baby, fall a-sleeping,
>   Lullaby, oh lullaby!

>   (442)

Mellifluous consonants and long vowels not only add resonance and melodiousness to the poem but at the same time slow the movement.

The lulling effect also results from the end-stopped lines, the caesuras, and the frequent use of words of which the sounds linger but do not run together. The meter, furthermore, produces a gentle rhythm. Though the opening syllable of each line is stressed, the prevailing foot is iambic. Each line (except for the refrain) has a feminine ending; however, the falling unstressed syllable combines with the stressed first syllable of the next line to give another slowly formed iambic foot. The smoothly controlled slow tempo supports the sound values of the poem. All these devices are coordinated to achieve tonal and structural unity and to produce the soporific effect appropriate to lullabies.

Many of the familiar objects and creatures from the natural world that are subjects of rhymes in "Mother Goose" are also found in *Sing-Song*. Numerous poems are about flowers, birds, animals, and especially small creatures such as frogs, toads, mice, and caterpillars. In most cases, Christina develops the country setting more extensively than in "Mother Goose" rhymes, and she shows a greater appreciation of the beauties of nature.

In *Sing-Song*, the wind is a favorite nature subject. One poem in particular is famous and is found in almost all anthologies of children's verse. It captures with childlike terseness the simple experience of observing the wind blowing through trees:

> Who has seen the wind?
>   Neither I nor you:
> But when the leaves hang trembling
>   The wind is passing thro'.
>
> Who has seen the wind?
>   Neither you nor I:
> But when the trees bow down their heads
>   The wind is passing by.
>
>   (438)

Another poem worth quoting from this general group is "Kookoorookoo":

> 'Kookoorookoo! kookoorookoo!'
>   Crows the cock before the morn;
> 'Kikirikee! kikirikee!'
>   Roses in the east are born.

> 'Kookoorookoo! kookoorookoo!'
> Early birds begin their singing;
> 'Kikirikee! kikirikee!'
> The day, the day, the day is
>   springing.

                                                                    (426)

The lilting music and rhythms used to herald a new day would delight any child, as would the sound made by the cock in spite of its difference from the conventional cock-adoodle-doo. William explained the peculiar crow of the cock as a reproduction of noises made by their father "to amuse his bantlings."

Still another pleasurable poem for children is "Lady Daffadowndilly":

> Growing in the vale
>   By the uplands hilly,
> Growing straight and frail,
>   Lady Daffadowndilly.
>
> In a golden crown,
>   And a scant green gown
> While the spring blows chilly,
>   Lady Daffadown,
> Sweet Daffadowndilly.

                                                                    (428)

Christina makes several significant changes from the version in "Mother Goose." Instead of having Daffadowndilly come to town, she keeps her in the country and develops the poem by adding nature images. These images and the special attention given to sound values stress the natural habitat of the daffodil in spring and the flower's delicate beauty.

Nonsense rhymes were found in early "Mother Goose" collections, but not many of them. It remained for Edward Lear with *Book of Nonsense* (1846) and for Lewis Carroll with *Alice's Adventure in Wonderland* (1865) to make popular the nonsense mode in children's literature. Both authors published again shortly before *Sing-Song:* Lear, *Nonsense Songs and Stories* (1871) and *More Nonsense Songs* (1872); Carroll, *Through the Looking Glass* (1871). Christina read Lear and Carroll and wrote a few nonsense verses for her volume. These are free adaptations of the limerick, such as

> If a pig wore a wig,
>   What could we say?
> Treat him as a gentleman,
>   And say 'Good-day.'
>
> If his tail chanced to fail,
>   What could we do? —
> Send him to the tailoress
>   To get one new.

                                                              (431)

Another is:

> When fishes set umbrellas up
>   If the rain-drops run,
> Lizards will want their parasols
>   To shade them from the sun.

                                                              (434)

In their works, Lear and Carroll were primarily concerned with entertaining children. Both writers gave free rein to the imagination and attempted to render the world of the child more authentically than was the practice of their contemporaries who were writing children's literature. In so doing, they were breaking with the didactic, moralistic, and sentimental tradition that the nineteenth century had inherited from the eighteenth. This tradition, which saw the child through adult eyes, continued throughout the nineteenth century, though it weakened considerably as the twentieth century approached.

In *Sing-Song*, the most characteristic poems continue the didactic and moral tradition. In fact, Barbara Garlitz shows that "half the poems in *Sing-Song* repeat the moral and sentimental themes which were the stock in trade of nineteenth-century children's poetry."[1] Among these are poems commending the virtues of humble country life, ones entreating children to be kind to birds and animals, and others urging sympathy for those less fortunate. Three poems suffice to illustrate the sentimental themes typical of *Sing-Song* as well as of contemporary children's verse:

> There's snow on the fields,
>   And cold in the cottage,
> While I sit in the chimney nook
>   Supping hot pottage.

My clothes are soft and warm,
  Fold upon fold,
But I'm so sorry for the poor
  Out in the cold.

(427)

Three little children
  On the wide wide earth,
Motherless children —
  Cared for from their birth
By tender angels.

Three little children
  On the wide wide sea.
Motherless children —
  Safe as safe can be
With guardian angels.

(436)

The dear old woman in the lane
  Is sick and sore with pains and aches,
We'll go to her this afternoon,
  And take her tea and eggs and cakes.

(440)

The poems on the theme of death — and there are many — tend to be moralistic and are undistinguished. Though Christina throughout her life was preoccupied with thoughts of death, the sentiment and point of view of these poems were also characteristic of nineteenth-century children's anthologies. In all likelihood, such poems had little appeal to her young readers; they certainly do not appeal to modern tastes, young or old. In any case, four of the poems about death concern babies, an example of which is the following:

A Baby's cradle with no baby in it,
  A baby's grave where autumn leaves
    drop sere;
The sweet soul gathered home to Paradise,
  The body waiting here.

(427)

This poem, like others on death and most of those intended for moral instruction, is written from the adult point of view. Poems in *Sing-Song* that project an adult's rather than a child's view of the

world seem today the least successful. One poem frequently singled
out to show how very unchildlike Christina can be is "I Planted a
Hand":

> I planted a hand
>   And there came up a palm,
> I planted a heart
>   And there came up balm.
>
> Then I planted a wish,
>   But there sprang a thorn,
> While heaven frowned with thunder
>   And earth sighed forlorn.

                                                                        (434)

In *Sing-Song*, when Christina moves away from moral themes and
away from the rigidly adult point of view, only then does she write
her most endearing poems. These are still being anthologized, and
they are still being enjoyed by children.

CHAPTER 8

Short Stories

I Commonplace

CHRISTINA published two collections of short stories, *Commonplace and Other Short Stories* (1870) for adult readers and *Speaking Likenesses* (1874) for children; but neither book proved very popular with the reading public. *Commonplace* contains eight stories, five of which had been published previously. The first-written one, "Nick," dates from 1852 or 1853; and the last, "Commonplace," was finished just prior to publication. The title story is a long drawn-out narrative about the Charlmont sisters, Jane, Lucy, and Catherine. Jane, the youngest, is quite beautiful but superficial and mercenary. She believes that money, not manners and morals, is what counts most in a husband. She succeeds in marrying George Durham, a foolish but wealthy man, and lives in luxury instead of love.

Lucy, almost thirty, has turned down several proposals of marriage because she thinks herself in love with Alan Hartley. When he marries another, she realizes that it is not really he she loves but rather a former rejected suitor, Arthur Tresham, who sincerely loves her. When Arthur proposes again, she accepts. Of this marriage, and in contrast to Jane's, the narrator says: "this time a true man and a true woman who loved and honoured each other . . . were joined together."[1] As for Catherine, the eldest, she remains a spinster who looks to a future with God.

Most of Christina's weaknesses as a storyteller appear in "Commonplace." She has trouble in maintaining strong narrative continuity, which is related to another difficulty, that of establishing a clear sense of time. The dialogue tends to be flat and unnatural, but she does portray characters with some distinctness. One voice, the narrator's, speaks through all the characters. And, finally, her style is uneven. The story contains poetic passages such as this one that describes a picnic site: "Rocky Drumble on a sunny summer-day was a bower of cool shade, and of a silence heightened, not broken, by sounds of birds and of water, the stream at hand, the sea not far off; a bower of sun-chequered shade, breaths of wind every moment shifting the shadows, and the sun making its way in, now here, now there, with an endless, monotonous changeableness."[2] But the story also contains colorless passages such as this: "As to the luncheon, it included everything usual and nothing unusual, and most of the company consuming it displayed fine, healthy appetites."[3]

Dante Gabriel referred to "Commonplace" as "the most everyday affair possible" but as not without some interest.[4] For those principally interested in biography, the story has special significance. The character of Lucy is, in part, a self-portrait; and Catherine is a close description of Maria. Other characters can be identified with people from the Rossetti social circle, and the scenes recall places visited by Christina.[5]

"The Lost Titian" tells the story of Titian, a recognized painter of masterpieces, and his friend Gianni, who is secondbest in his endeavors. In a card game, Gianni wins Titian's latest masterpiece, one not yet unveiled to the public; and he paints a dragon picture over it to hide the original. After Titian's death, he intends to declare it as his own. However, he loses the painting to another gambler. He then paints a second and superior dragon picture in hopes of ransoming the first, but he himself dies before he can recover it. The ironic turnabout is complete and the moral clear: Gianni's envy gains him nothing. Many critics consider "The Lost Titian" the most effectively told of all the stories in the collection. The action moves along steadily and quickly to its climax. Characters are rather deftly drawn, and the reader feels some tension between them. A rich and sensuous atmosphere pervades the story.

Two of the stories, "Nick" and "Hero," are cast in the form of fairy tales, a form with which Christina felt comfortable because it allowed for freer use of her imagination. Like "The Lost Titian," both these tales teach a lesson about envy. In the first, Nick, though possessing all of the material things necessary to satisfy his wants, is "discontented and envious." When a "little rosy woman, no bigger than a butterfly" gives him the opportunity of becoming everything he wishes, he undergoes a series of transformations, all of which permit him to vent his resentments and envy on other people. In turn, he becomes a flight of sparrows, a cat, a dog, a bludgeon, a fire, and a rich old man. None of his experiences while metamorphosed, however, bring him any happiness. His final wish returns him to his former self, but he is now cleansed of all envy. Though emphatically made, the moral is not obtrusive. A profusion of details creates an effective illusion of reality, and the naiveté in tone characteristic of traditional fairy tales is achieved here.

In "Hero," the protagonist is "stung by supposed indifference" and becomes selfish. One day, while walking along the shore, she discovers that the Princess Royal has drifted from Fairyland across the waters to man-side. Agreeing to return her to Fairyland, Hero is granted one most desired wish: "to become the supreme object of admiration." To have the wish fulfilled, Hero must first go to Fairyland; and there her body is kept while her spirit, enshrined in a diamond, is cast ashore man-side and soon found. As an "incomparable diamond," she is given supreme admiration; but she also causes greed, warfare, and death. After several adventures, Hero longs for her old way of life; and she is eventually returned via Fairyland to her lover and her father. She marries and lives happily, often telling her children of the marvels of Fairyland. She always concludes her story with these words: "though admiration seems sweet at first, only love is sweet first, and last and always."[6]

The handling of time in "Hero" is awkward and confusing, but the problem is not too disturbing because of the fairy-tale subject. All things considered, the story is enjoyable. Dante Gabriel, who thought it "splendid," wrote to Christina that she "ought to write more such things."[7] Of special merit are the delightful descriptions of Fairyland, such as the following: "A hum, a buzz, voices singing and speaking, the splash of fountains, airy laughter, rustling wings, the noise of a thousand leaves and flowercups in commotion. Sparks dancing in the twilight, dancing feet, joy and triumph; unseen hands loosing succous, interlacing stalks from their roots beneath the water; towing a lily-raft across the lake, down a tortuous inland creek, through Fairy-harbour, out into the open sea."[8]

The remaining stories have little to distinguish them. "Vanna's Twins" is a tragic tale of a Neapolitan couple and their twin children. While on an errand of mercy, the two children become lost in a snowstorm and perish; and, heartbroken, the couple decide to return to Italy. Unlike "Vanna's Twins," "A Safe Investment" is an allegory. One dark ominous night a stranger rides into a town, and he finds turmoil everywhere. The gas works explode, ships with their cargoes sink in the harbor, the treasurer of the railroad absconds with funds, and the banks fail. The stranger speaks with the people, all of whom are bewailing the loss of their investments. So totally preoccupied are they with their material ruin that no one offers the stranger any hospitality, except one woman who receives him into her humble cottage. She tells him: "My money . . . is not invested as so many in this town have invested theirs. When I was yet young, One told me that riches do certainly make to themselves wings and fly away; and that gold perisheth, though it be purified seven times in the fire."[9] Her time is spent in acts of mercy. In the morning the stranger leaves, and the narrator concludes the story: "Whence he came and whither he went I know not, but he rode as one that carries back tidings to Him that sent him. Also this I know, that some, being mindful to entertain strangers, have entertained angels unawares."[10]

The last two stories in the collection also have for their main purpose the illustration of religious views. "Pros and Cons" is based on an actual incident, an attempt by the rector of Christina's parish church to abolish pew rents. In the story, the rector, Mr. Goodman, debates the issue in the rectory drawing room with a number of his parishioners. His proposal is made in the hope of carrying out the Christian doctrine, "of our absolute equality before God," but all of his arguments are ineffectual. In disgust, he exclaims: "I avow that you, my brethren, have this evening furnished me with the only plausible argument in favour of pews which has ever been suggested to me, for it *is* hard upon our open-hearted poor that they should be compelled to sit by persons who, instead of viewing them as brethren beloved, despise the poor."[11] "Pros and Cons" is not in any technical sense a short story, but the dramatized incident does present forcefully the hypocritical response of churchgoers to a doctrine of Christian teaching.

The action of "The Waves of This Troublesome World" is more complicated than in "Pros and Cons," but the doctrinal content that is stressed with equal determination concerns the parable of the lost sheep. Sarah Lane, the lost sheep, has strayed from the true church by marrying a Methodist. For this act she is ostracized by family and friends. Years later, her husband and son dead, she is shown kindness by the curate's wife who slowly reindoctrinates her until she is again received into the church; and, as a result, "there is joy in the presence of the angels of God over one sinner that repenteth." The story itself functions as a parable to illustrate a parable; but, being overly concerned with the presenting of theological views,

Christina fails to achieve an effective fusion of theme and narrative elements.

Dante Gabriel was undeniably right when he wrote Christina that her "proper business" was "to write poetry, and not *Commonplaces*."[12] Though she repeated many times that she could not at will bid the muse of poetry to speak, the writing of poetry evidently came more naturally to her than the creation of prose fiction. At any rate, in 1891 when she sent a list of her works to Patchett Martin, who was preparing an article about her, she added this note beside *Commonplace and Other Short Stories*: "Out of print and not worth reprinting."[13]

II Speaking Likenesses

Considering the general acclaim given *Sing-Song* upon its publication in 1872, one would have expected Christina to follow its success with another book of children's poetry. Instead, she published *Speaking Likenesses*, a collection of three tales for children. She dedicated the book to her mother "in grateful remembrance of the stories with which she used to entertain her children." Arthur Hughes, whose delightful illustrations helped make *Sing-Song* a success, also illustrated *Speaking Likenesses*. Christina regarded the work as a "Christmas trifle" written in the "*Alice* style with an eye to the market."[14] She hoped to take advantage of the vogue for children's literature created in great part by Edward Lear and Lewis Carroll and, to some extent, by herself. Her attitude here is contrary to the general impression of her as a writer all but oblivious to the outside world. Indeed, in other instances regarding her publications she showed considerable sensitivity to the "buying public" and concern for her fame as an author.

The original title of *Speaking Likenesses* was "Nowhere," but Dante Gabriel convinced her that it ought to be changed because of its similarity to Samuel Butler's anagrammatically titled and "freethinking" novel *Erewhon*, published in 1872. Apparently Alexander Macmillan, her publisher, had reservations about the appropriateness or attractiveness of the title; for Christina, in defending it, wrote him: "And then I really must adopt 'Speaking Likenesses' as my title, this having met with some approval in my circle. Very likely you did not so deeply ponder upon my text as to remark that my small heroines perpetually encounter 'speaking (literally *speaking*) likenesses' or embodiments or caricatures of themselves or their faults. This premised, I think the title boasts of some point &

neatness."[15] Christina's defense stresses her didactic intention in writing the tales.

The three tales are held together by a narrative frame: an aunt gathers her five nieces about her and narrates the stories. While she knits, four of the girls sew, and the other draws. This realistic framework is maintained principally by having the children interrupt the stories from time to time to ask questions and by providing conversational links between the tales. The aunt replies to these questions and pauses occasionally herself to offer brief moralizing comments on the characters and the action.

In the first story, Flora is celebrating her eighth birthday with her brother, sister, and five guests. Instead of playing happily, the children bicker over who took the biggest sugar plum, create a disturbance at dinner and are dissatisfied with the food, and in general spend the time squabbling. During the games which follow dinner — blindman's buff, hide-and-seek, and running across the sloping lawn — Flora is disconsolate because the children are not deferring to her wishes even though it is her birthday. Finally, she sullenly wanders off alone and, growing weary, falls asleep. In a dream, she finds herself standing before a door; the knocker shakes hands with her; the bell handle opens the door; she enters a strange room:

All the chairs were stuffed arm-chairs, and moved their arms and shifted their shoulders to accommodate sitters. All the sofas arranged and rearranged their pillows as convenience dictated. Footstools glided about, and rose or sank to meet every length of leg. Tables were no less obliging, but ran on noiseless castors here or there when wanted. Tea-trays ready set out, saucers of strawberries, jugs of cream, and plates of cake, floated in, settled down, and floated out again empty, with considerable tact and good taste. . . . Photographs and pictures made the tour of the apartment, standing still when glanced at and going on when done with. In case of need the furniture flattened itself against the wall, and cleared the floor for a game, or I dare say for a dance.[16]

The contrast between the obliging nature of the animated objects in the room and the pouting, grumbling, unaccommodating children at Flora's party is apparent.

As Flora sees herself reflected in the mirrors that cover the walls and the ceiling, she becomes extremely self-conscious. The effect, in fact, of the whole dream sequence, in contrast with real life, is to make her painfully aware of her own faults and also of those of the many boys and girls who now fill the room. When she takes up a spoon with strawberries and cream, the selfish queen of the feast, who is Flora's counterpart, screams, "You shan't, they're mine." There follows a description of the children as "embodiments" of the main faults of the children at Flora's own party: "One boy bristled with prickly quills like a porcupine, and raised or depressed them at pleasure; but he usually kept them pointed outwards. Another instead of being rounded like most people was facetted at very sharp angles. A third caught in everything he came near, for he was hung round with hooks like fishhooks. One girl exuded a sticky fluid and came off on the fingers; another, rather smaller, was slimy and slipped through the hands."[17] The didactic-minded aunt observes that "such exceptional features could not but prove inconvenient, yet patience and forbearance might still have done something towards keeping matters smooth."[18]

A battle of the sexes follows upon Flora's suggestion that they play "Les Grâces," a girl's game. The queen, however, insists that Hunt the Pincushion be played and that Flora be the pincushion. So the children stick her full of pins. Again the aunt informs her listeners that the children hurt themselves as much as they hurt Flora and that, though all this happens in the "Land of Nowhere," it could happen in the "Land of Somewhere." The next game is "Self Help," a free-for-all in which the children attack each other, the boys taking special delight in annoying the girls.

By now, Flora begins to change her behavior. At supper, everyone except Flora greedily stuffs himself. Afterward the children construct on the playground individual houses of "brick-shaped pieces of glass." In his glass house, each child is seen in his most unflattering aspect; and, following a name-calling session, a stone-throwing fight breaks out. Flora, who was housed with the queen, is in a frenzy and vainly tries to stop the turmoil. At this point in her dream, she awakens and joins her guests at tea. Having learned her lesson, she is full of remorse for having been cross. The story ends with the aunt's drawing the moral: "And I think if she [Flora] lives to be nine years old and give another birthday party, she is likely on that occasion to be even less like the birthday Queen of her troubled dream than was the Flora of eight years old: who, with dear friends and playmates and pretty presents, yet scarcely knew how to bear a few trifling disappointments, or how to be obliging and good-humoured under slight annoyances."[19]

The second tale is without the violence or heavy didacticism of the first, but it is hardly more delightful; indeed, it must be regarded as a dull "trifle." The story concerns a little girl named Edith who tries in vain to light a fire to heat a kettle for a planned gypsy tea in the beech woods. The setting is of some interest for children because a group of forest creatures are brought together as spectators and as would-be helpers for the task at hand. Along with the girl's dog, cat, and cockatoo, the gathering includes a squirrel, a pair of wood pigeons, a mole, a toad, two hedgehogs, a frog, and an Aesopian fox, who, unable to reach the lowest bunch of grapes, goes off muttering, "They must be sour." Eventually the nurse arrives to light the fire and to send Edith back to the house. Christina might have exploited here her own delight in small animals, but she does little to enliven the story.

The third story is about Maggie, the orphaned granddaughter of Dame Margaret, who is the proprietor of the village fancy shop and who helps needy persons — except for undeserving idlers and drunkards. On Christmas Eve, Maggie offers to deliver a package to the doctor's house on the other side of the forest some distance from the village. Immediately upon setting out, Maggie falls and bumps her head. She continues on her way, but from that moment "commenced her marvellous adventures." She first encounters a group of children sporting about like grasshoppers that "leaped over oaks, wrestled in mid-air, bounded past a dozen trees at once; two and two they spun round like whirlwinds; they darted straight up like balloons; they tossed each other about like balls."[20] Maggie would play with them, but they cannot agree on a game, and she realizes her duty to deliver the package.

She next runs from a boy who had "arms, legs, a head, like ordinary people; but his face exhibited only one feature; and that was a wide mouth." Now growing drowsy, she comes upon a group of people yawning and sleeping round a fire. She resists the temptation to rest, resolutely trudging on until she reaches the doctor's door. But she is not asked in; so, "chilled to the bone, famished, cross, and almost fit to cry with disappointment," she wearily starts homeward. Her mood is brightened when she befriends a wood pigeon, a tabby kitten, and a puppy, all of which she takes home. Her grandmother welcomes her; and, after some tea, everyone is made cozy and goes to sleep.

The story of Flora's birthday is subject to Freudian interpretation, but, as Packer observes, the "strain of morbidity" can be accounted for rather simply by Christina's poor health during 1870–72.[21] Though such matters concern the special reader interested in biography, today the general reader, both young and old, probably finds little to enjoy in the tale of Flora or in the tales of Edith and Maggie. The author's didactic purpose of displaying child behavior when most unpleasant as judged by adults is much too bluntly handled. Christina overlooked, in explaining the title to Macmillan, another rather obvious significance of the word "likenesses": that, by improving their conduct, children would become likenesses of their parents; they would indeed emulate adult behavior but as ideally conceived by adults themselves. Such was the point of view from which most of the children's literature was written in the nineteenth century until Lear and Carroll gave impetus to the view that pleasure ought to be its major and perhaps sole purpose. Few children gain pleasure or actual benefit from the stern moralizing of adults who demand "adult" rather than childlike behavior of them.

Though Christina asserted that *Speaking Likenesses* was in the *Alice* style, her book falls far short of its model. As one critic (of many) has pointed out, "the charm of Alice was, and still is, that she is a real little girl, exploring the land of wonder, not that of reward and punishment for goodness or naughtiness."[22] Flora and the other children in *Speaking Likenesses* are by intent caricatures of faults or virtues; and what wonders we have are forced into service for this purpose. One of the aunt's listeners begs her, after hearing the first two tales, to be "wonderful" in the third story. The aunt replies, "I will try to be wonderful; but I cannot promise first-rate wonders on such extremely short notice."[23] In the final analysis, the chief disappointment in these tales is that they contain no "first-rate wonders," only first-rate moralizing.

CHAPTER 9

Religious Prose

CHRISTINA'S religious prose gives one little reason for thinking that it was written by anyone except a person who found it
easy to accept biblical teachings and who had a steadfast faith in
biblical consolations and promises. The doubts and tensions, the
painful dichotomized struggle between flesh and spirit, in short, the
sufferings of a distressed soul that are given expression in much of
her poetry are seen in the prose, when seen at all, as though in calm
retrospect. The great emotional drama of the poetry is absent,
therefore, from her prose prayers and commentary. By about 1874,
the date of her first religious prose work, *Annus Domini*, Christina
seems to have resolved her spiritual problems. The resolution —
though not a complete or necessarily happy one — was effected by
her adopting an attitude that enabled her to set forth her religious
views without greatly engaging her emotions. Whereas her secular
poetry represents an attempt at applying Christian precepts to the
practical and emotional realities of life, her religious prose (and most
of her later religious poetry) represents an articulation of these
precepts as a mental construct. In this articulation, she indulges in
very little intellectualizing because analyzing and questioning are
unnecessary. However, the result, as readers have observed, is a
piety that appears too self-conscious.

I Annus Domini

The nature of *Annus Domini* is indicated by the subtitle: *A Prayer
for Each Day of the Year, Founded on a Text of Holy Scripture*. In a
brief introduction to the first edition, H. W. Burrows observes that
the prayers are "valuable in themselves from their fervour,
reverence, and overflowing charity, and also because they are suggestive of the use which should be made of Holy Scripture in our
devotions."[1]

A poem of thirteen three-line stanzas (titled "Wrestling" in *The*

Poetical Works) that precedes the prose prayers gives the general theme of the volume as a whole — the need to make oneself worthy of Christ's bountiful mercy and love. All the prayers are addressed to Christ and beseech His grace to enable one to avoid the temptations of the world and to devote one's life to adoring Jesus, God the Father, and the Holy Spirit. Parallel structure, balanced phrasing, antithesis, and pronounced rhythm give Christina's style some of the poetic qualities found in the Bible. A typical example is Prayer 45, based on the text from Psalm XVIII, 3:

"O Lord Jesus Christ, Worthy to be praised, give us grace, I beseech Thee, to attribute no good thing to ourselves; not desiring the praise of men, or puffing up our neighbour with vain flatteries, but ascribing all praise unto Thee on Whom praise waiteth: for Thou alone, O Lord Jesus, with Thy Father and Thy Holy Spirit, art worthy of the blessing and thanksgiving, worship and magnifying, adoration and love, of Cherubim and Seraphim, Angels and Archangels, men and all creatures. Amen"

In compactness and imagistic power some of the prayers are comparable to Christina's best poetry: "O Lord Jesus Christ, Lily of the Valleys, clothe us, I beseech Thee, in whiteness of purity, greenness of hope, fragrance of prayer: and grant that no enemy may pluck us out of thy Hand" (Prayer 101).

Though *Annus Domini* was intended as a prayer book appropriate to the spiritual needs of all Christians, the prayers reflect more particularly Christina's personal struggle for spirituality, and Prayer 103 is one of these: "O Lord Jesus Christ, our Shadow from the heat when the blast of the terrible ones is as a storm against the wall, save us, I implore Thee, under all stress of terrible temptation. Deliver us from rebellion of passion, seduction of the flesh, allurements of the world, provocations of the devil: deliver us from siege and from surprise, from our foes and from ourselves, O Lord, Amen." In composing the prayer, Christina no doubt had in mind her own efforts throughout life to subdue her passionate nature, to deny all that appeared tainted with worldliness, and to maintain psychic and emotional harmony. This prayer, however, and others like it lack the feverishness and the strong sense of immediacy that characterize many of her poems of spiritual crisis.

II   Seek and Find

Christina's second religious prose work, *Seek and Find*, was published in 1879 under the direction of the Tract Committee of the

Society for Promoting Christian Knowledge. Thereafter the Society published all of her religious prose. *Seek and Find* includes two series of commentary on the Benedicite, the Song of the Three Young Men which forms part of one of the Additions to Daniel in the Apocrypha. One series is about creation; the other, about redemption. The works and creatures of God as praise-givers are listed, and then follows the commentary that is lavishly sprinkled with quotations and paraphrases from the Bible. Because of Christina's intimate knowledge of the Bible, she writes with confidence and brings together almost imperceptibly her ideas and those of her source.

In a letter to Dante Gabriel, Christina observed of the prose of *Seek and Find:* "I flatter myself some of it is that prose which I fancy our Italian half inclines us to indite."[2] In turn, Dante Gabriel noted that, though the work was "full of eloquent beauties," it was "most seriously damaged . . . by the confusion of references with the text, which they completely smother."[3] Her commentaries on natural phenomena have a half-scientific, half-poetic cast; and her canticle on the wind, for example, closely combines her rhetoric with that of the Bible's: "Precious and beneficent is wind in the material world. It stirs us, purifies, winnows, casts aside: it is antagonistic to stagnation, to corruption: it brings heat, and likewise cold; it carries clouds, and dries up humidity. Invisible, intangible, audible, sensible, it has a breath so gentle as scarcely to bend a flower, and a blast stronger than the strength of the sea (Ex. xiv. 21), stronger than the strength of the solid earth (1 Kings xix. 11)."[4]

One of Christina's objectives in *Seek and Find*, as well as in her other religious prose works, is to demonstrate the essential unity of the Old and New Testaments. Other contemporary religious writers were concerned with the same thing; in fact, as Gisela Hönnighausen points out, "the attempt to prove harmony in the Gospels and the prefigurative interpretation of the Old Testament, which betrays a specific form of medieval thought, reached a new peak in Christina Rossetti's time." She further observes: "It may seem strange that at a time when criticism of the Bible was employing scientific arguments to query the truth of it, medieval methods were being used to interpret the Bible. This retreat into the thought of a previous century, suggested by the tradition of Romantic medievalism, is understandable in the light of the philosophical crisis of the nineteenth century which made the certainty provided by earlier absolute faith seem desirable."[5]

As a reaction to these concerns of her era, Christina's *Seek and*

Find is a main source of information about her attitudes toward biology, geology, astronomy, and other fields in which new theories challenged and often disturbed Victorian thinkers. She discusses doctrines of evolution and theories of creation, and she reveals considerable knowledge of the Higher Criticism of the Bible, particularly that which deals with the time span during creation as given in Genesis. The nineteenth century, she writes,

seems beyond all previous centuries to be a period of running to and fro, and of increased knowledge (see Dan. xiii. 4). Now therefore presumably, in at any rate no less a degree than heretofore, must men be liable to the risk of at once knowing and not knowing; knowing many things, while ignoring the one thing needful (see St. Luke x. 41, 42); adding knowledge to knowledge, but not as St. Peter bids us adding it to virtue, and least of all adding it through virtue to underlying faith (2 St. Pet. 1. 5).[6]

In general, she sees no conflict between science and religion; and she attributes man's problems to his ignorance and to his lack of faith in the infinite creative powers and wisdom of God. "We can make of what we know and of what we know not," she says, "stepping-stones towards heaven."[7] She insists, finally, that both the known and the unknown must be celebrated in the name of God.

III Called to be Saints

Called to be Saints is a hagiography which was published in 1881, but it had been offered earlier to Macmillan and had been rejected in 1876. Appropriately, it was dedicated to Maria "In Hope of Our Re-Union," for Christina always regarded her sister as a saint. The aim of the work is given in the "Key": "I will endeavour to write of the nineteen Saints commemorated by name in our Book of Common Prayer, with the Holy Innocents neither named nor numbered, with St. Michael and his cloud of All Angels, with All Saints as the stars of the firmament and as the sand by the sea-shore innumerable. . . ."[8] For each saint she gives biblical extracts, "biographical addition," prayers of her own, and then describes flowers and gems deemed appropriate. The style of the biographies and prayers is stately and sonorous, much like that of *Annus Domini*, of the King James Bible, and of the prose of two great religious writers of earlier centuries, Richard Hooker and Thomas Fuller.

Flowers and precious stones serve as emblems for certain qualities of the saints. This emblematic use of objects of nature — that is, the attributing special significance to them by way of pointing a moral

— is a characteristic of Christina's religious prose and poetry.[9] For example, the opening line of the poem, "Consider the Lilies of the Field," is explicit in reminding the reader that "Flowers preach to us if we will hear." The didactic purpose for using emblems is closely related to Christina's sacramental view, a view that characterized the medieval religious mind and continued into the nineteenth century as an important aspect of the traditional Christian's way of looking at the natural world. One was expected to look behind the merely physical to spiritual manifestations, all of which emanate from one Godhead. Christina's emblem writing is an interesting feature of *Called to be Saints*.

IV Letter and Spirit

Letter and Spirit was published in 1883 and was dedicated to Christina's mother "In Thankfulness For Her Dear and Honoured Example." A work of extended commentary on the Ten Commandments, *Letter and Spirit* points out parallels and interrelationships between the Commandments. Special attention is given to ways of achieving unity in life by living the Great Commandment (Matthew 22:34-40 and Mark 12: 28-31) proclaimed by Christ of loving God and neighbor. Ultimate unity in God, however, will come on the day of the Last Judgment. In the meantime, what counts is not so much obedience to the letter of the law as written on stone but the practice of the spirit of the law as written in men's hearts. A final recommendation is made to remember always to turn to the "Supreme Example" of one who truly lived a life of love: "And now since one example is worth a world of precepts, let us briefly contemplate the winning Perfection of our dear Lord: Who while going in and out among his fellow-men condescended to fulfil before their eyes and in their ears the Law of Love; making Himself, as it were, God's Epistle written in our very hearts, known and read of all Christians to all generations."[10]

V Time Flies

Time Flies, published in 1885, is for the general reader perhaps Christina's most interesting prose writing; for it is, as Packer notes, "Christina's only attempt at informal autobiography."[11] Dedicated to her mother, again as her "Beloved Example," the work is subtitled *A Reading Diary;* and it affords a more varied and directly personal look at Christina than anything else she wrote. Feast Days or little incidents from her life or from her friends' lives serve as occasions for drawing lessons for improvement of one's Christian character. Little prose or poetic sermons for each day of the year are on a wide range of subjects: patience, puns, music, tact, sloth, death, false etymology, love of enemies, resignation, and a host of other topics.

Under the January 3 date, for example, she writes of scrupulosity and then applies the remarks to herself:

Scrupulous persons, — a much tried and much trying sort of people, looked up to and looked down upon by their fellows.

Sometimes paralysed and sometimes fidgeted by conscientiousness, they are often in the way yet often not at hand.

The main pity is that they do not amend themselves. Next to this, it is a pity when they gratuitously attempt what under the circumstances they cannot perform.

Listen to an anecdote or even to a reminiscence from their lips, and you are liable to hear an exercise on possible contingencies: a witticism hangs fire, a heroic example is dwarfed by modifying suggestions. Eloquence stammers in their mouth, the thread even of logic is snapped.

Their aim is to be accurate; a worthy aim: but do they achieve accuracy? Such handling as blunts the pointed and flattens the lofty cannot boast of accuracy.

These remarks have, I avow, a direct bearing on my own case.[12]

This passage supports William Michael's contention in the "Memoir" that Christina's character was marred by overscrupulousness. But the passage also calls attention to what must be regarded as an admirable trait of character — Christina's high degree of self-awareness. Indeed, this self-awareness that emanates from much of her work, especially her poetry, gives it warmth and genuineness.

In addition to rather grave moral instruction in *Time Flies*, Christina offers such pedestrian advice as the following:

A bad beginning may be retrieved and a good ending achieved. No beginning, no ending.[13]

Can a pun profit? Seldom, I fear. Puns and such like are a frivolous crew likely to misbehave unless kept within strict bonds.[14]

Whether the instruction in *Time Flies* is given in short poems, apothegms, or in solemn expansive prose, the reader's main interest in the work is in the personal insights it offers into Christina's character.

VI The Face of the Deep: A Devotional
Commentary on the Apocalypse

In *The Face of the Deep: A Devotional Commentary on the Apocalypse*, published in 1892, the dedication is to the "cherished Memory" of Christina's mother, whom she acknowledges in the prefatory note as having "once pointed out to me Patience as our lesson in the Book of Revelations." She adds that, "if any deign to seek Patience in my company, I pray them to remember that One high above me in the Kingdom of Heaven heads our pilgrim caravan," and she concludes with a short poem on patience.[15]

Her method is to cite verse from the Apocalypse and then to offer commentary interspersed with scriptural quotations and personal poetry. "I work at prose," she said while writing *The Face of the Deep*, "and help myself forward with little bits of verse."[16] Actually, her prose moves along rapidly, even at times in a headlong fashion. The Apocalypse she knew intimately, it being her favorite part of the Bible; and her mind apparently is overflowing with things she wants to say about it. As she rushes along, she drifts almost effortlessly into prayers, of which the following is an example: "O Gracious Saviour, Who bestowedst upon St. John a great glory of humility when he bare record how Thou saidst not of him, 'He shall not die,' grant unto us in mortal life humility, and in life immortal glory."[17]

In this prayer, as in most of her prayers or poem-prayers, the keynote is humility. With her strong sense of unworthiness, she tried never to be presumptuous in approaching God through prayer. Always on guard against the sins of self-righteousness and pride, she kept ever in mind the biblical precept that "whosoever exalteth himself shall be abased; and he that humbleth himself shall be exalted." In writing to Dante Gabriel a few months before his death, Christina cited the following couplet by Isaac Williams as one to which "I thoroughly assent": " 'Tis like frail man to love to walk on high, / But to be lowly is to be like God."[18]

That the last work published before Christina's own death on December 29, 1894, should have been a commentary on the Apocalypse is indeed fitting. None of the books of the Bible more profoundly influenced her life and writings than the Book of Revelation. From youth to old age, through many years of infirmity, her hope for happiness — though wavering and unconsoling at times —

rested on the apocalyptic promises in the Book of Revelation. And appropriately in taking humble leave of the reader at the close of *The Face of the Deep* she says, perhaps again recalling Isaac Williams' lines: "If I have been overbold in attempting such a work as this, I beg pardon."[19]

CHAPTER 10

Achievement

THE literature of the Victorian period is characterized by great diversity. Certainly many of the writers of the period have features in common, but the significant differences between writers and the variety in the canons of individual authors are what give the literature its vitality. Such is the case with Christina Rossetti. Even though much of her work can be related to that of others, her voice is authentically her own; and her total achievement is surprisingly diverse. She wrote over a thousand poems and more than eight volumes of prose. The poetry ranges from sensuous Pre-Raphaelite to ascetic devotional and includes some charming verse for children. The prose ranges from short stories for children and adults to formal prayers and religious commentary and includes an instructional diary. Not all of her accomplishments are worthy of acclaim, but several are of unquestionable merit and deserve recognition in the literary history of the latter half of the nineteenth century.

Christina's connection with the Pre-Raphaelite Movement must be acknowledged. Some of her early poetry is in the Keats-Tennyson tradition and has affinities with the work of poets who came to be identified as Pre-Raphaelites. Although not a formal member of the Pre-Raphaelite Brotherhood when it was founded in 1848, she was nonetheless closely associated with it mainly through her two brothers, and seven of her poems appeared in issues of its journal. Moreover, in 1862 her first collection of poetry, *Goblin Market and Other Poems,* received considerable public and critical attention, whereas earlier published works of the Pre-Raphaelites Dante Gabriel Rossetti, William Morris, and Algernon Swinburne went virtually unnoticed.

After the publication of Christina's next volume, *The Prince's Progress and Other Poems,* in 1866, her reputation was firmly established. The title poems of these volumes are distinctly Pre-

Raphaelite, and "Goblin Market" is justly famous as one of Christina's most original achievements and as an outstanding example of Pre-Raphaelite verse. Many later poems also contain Pre-Raphaelite characteristics, most notably a rich textured pictorial effect, sensuous details used for mood evocation, and a combining of concrete imagery with abstract elements to produce a semimystical quality. But the development of her poetic vision did not take her in the direction of escaping into a medieval past or utopian future, or of the aestheticism that marked Pre-Raphaelitism in the closing decades of the century. Her strong tendency, however, to internalize experience, to write little spiritual autobiographies in verse, associates her with the main thrust of Romanticism. Furthermore, her concern with intimate moods, ones emotionally and imaginatively projected, gives much of her best poetry modern appeal.

Christina was the most widely read writer of religious verse in her day, and she must be regarded as one of the major religious poets in English. Along with a notable array of nineteenth-century Anglo-Catholic and Catholic poets such as John Keble, John Henry Newman, Coventry Patmore, and Gerard Manley Hopkins, who wrote under the stimulus of the Oxford Movement, she helped to revitalize the tradition of orthodox religious verse and to advance it into the post-Victorian period. Modern readers, it is true, are more attracted to the dynamic quality and verbal virtuosity of Hopkins than to the more conventional Christina, but for many of her contemporary readers her devotional poetry served as a means of reaffirming Church doctrines and Christian values and of nourishing hope in an age of weakening faith.

Of lesser significance than Christina's devotional verse but still deserving mention is her religious prose. It does not bear comparison with the work of the eminent Victorian prose writers who discussed critical issues of the day for a public audience; but her prose, much more limited in scope, did meet the devotional needs of Christian readers. Though heavily dependent on the Bible for inspiration and sentiment, her religious prose contains interesting personal touches and imaginative elements. The style is formal with long, involuted sentences, balanced phrasing, and Latinate diction; and the sonorous tones and strong rhythms are reminiscent of the King James Bible, of the writings of Richard Hooker, and of Thomas Fuller. The effect, overall, is one of stateliness and dignity. The religious prose belongs to a minor genre, for its origin goes back to the devotional literature of the medieval period and to the sixteenth and early seventeenth centuries, but the genre enjoyed renewed popularity in the nineteenth century.

In the history of children's poetry, Christina's place is secure. "Goblin Market" won immediate contemporary success and has since attained the stature of a classic. One of the great poems of fancy in English, "Goblin Market" is also one of those rare poems that can be enjoyed by adults as well as by children. *Sing-Song* was a representative collection in 1872, for it looked back to older modes and forward to newer ones. The sentimental, didactic and moralistic poems continued the older tradition; and, though they found favor with readers in Christina's day, they have slight appeal today. The nonsense rhymes that strengthened the newer light verse tradition of Edward Lear and Lewis Carroll are occasionally reprinted today. The nonmoralistic poems, however, proved the most memorable. Often subtle in melody and mood, they are a link with the artistic masterpieces in *Songs of Innocence* by William Blake and of those by Walter de la Mare and other modern authors whose poetry displays childlike qualities. Such poems as "What is Pink?" "Who Has Seen the Wind?" and "Lullaby, oh Lullaby" by Christina are still being read with delight by children and praised by critics.

Christina's highest achievement is undoubtedly her non-devotional poems, and they bring her into the mainstream of dialectic poetry in the Victorian period. In these, whether religious or secular in context, she probes deeply into her personality, revealing the tortured soul of a sensitive poet who deprived herself of earthly pleasures but did so with regrets that she could not fully suppress. They frequently express a wavering faith that led to an agonizing sense of unworthiness and even of alienation from God. Her doubts, anxieties, and despair are akin to those of other poets who were distressed by the loss of belief in traditional religious and social values. In her case, however, she writes not so much in intellectual reaction to the perplexing ideas in the world as in emotional reaction to her own personal situation. Nonetheless, many of her tones and techniques are those found in the work of the major poets of her day. That she lacks the emotional and musical variety of Tennyson, the intellectual depth and dramatic vibrancy of Browning, and the philosophic sweep of Arnold can be admitted without being apologetic. For among her canon are many lyrics dealing with crises of the human spirit that equal in power and technical skill those of her more celebrated contemporaries.

Looked at as a whole, Christina Rossetti's poetry records her search — which in truth is everyone's search — to know herself and to find meaning in life. More particularly, as a Christian she was dismayed at the irreconcilability of the seemingly opposed values of the temporal world in which she lived and the spiritual world to which she aspired. The consequence was a terrible inner conflict. Though she might accept in her mind the doctrines of her professed religion, she could not calmly dismiss the yearnings of her heart or the cravings of the senses. Such a condition is the essence of Christian tragedy. Such a condition resulted in the creation of her greatest poetry. In its myth-making tendency to depict states of mind, in its intensity, and in its honesty, this poetry elevates personal experience to the universal level and earns her a place among the significant poets of the nineteenth century.

Notes and References

Chapter One

1. From the Diary of William M. Rossetti, "Appendix," *The Family Letters of Christina Georgina Rossetti*, ed. William Michael Rossetti (1908; reprint. New York, 1968), p. 213.

2. *The Poetical Works of Christina Georgina Rossetti*, ed. William Michael Rossetti (London, 1904). Hereafter cited as *Works*. Page numbers for poetry quoted from this edition appear in parentheses immediately after quotations.

3. *Dante Gabriel Rossetti: His Family Letters, With a Memoir*, ed. William Michael Rossetti (London, 1895) I, 22.

4. Ibid., II, 297.

5. Christina probably read *The Imitation of Christ* in the English translation of Richard Whitford (c. 1476–1555). *The Imitation* in this translation was widely read throughout the nineteenth century. For information about Richard and Thomas, I am indebted to the introduction by Harold C. Gardiner, S. J., to his modern version of *The Imitation of Christ* (New York, 1955). The quoted phrase is Gardiner's.

6. *Works*, p. lxix.

7. Christina's two articles on Dante are "Dante, an English Classic," *Churchman's Shilling Magazine* 2 (1867), 200–5, and "Dante. The Poet Illustrated out of the Poem," *The Century* 27, n.s. 5 (Feb., 1884), 566–73.

8. William Sharp, "Some Reminiscences of Christina Rossetti," *The Atlantic Monthly* 75 (June, 1895), 740. The title of Maria's book is *A Shadow of Dante: Being an Essay Towards Studying Himself, His World and His Pilgrimage*.

Chapter Two

1. "A Few Words to the Reader," G. Polidori in *Verses* by Christina G. Rossetti (London, 1847).

2. *Maude: A Story for Girls*, Introduction, William Michael Rossetti (London, 1897), pp. 53–54.

3. Ibid., p. 57.

4. *Works*, p. 460. In all, eight poems not in the English edition were included in an American edition (Chicago, 1897). Perhaps they were left out because of copyright restrictions, or perhaps William Michael preferred to omit at least some of them because of their gloomy tone.

5. *The Family Letters of Christina Georgina Rossetti*, Letter dated Aug. 25, 1849, pp. 5–6.

6. *Maude*, pp. viii–x.

7. *The Germ* (London, 1901; reprint. New York, 1965), p. 6.

8. Ibid., 2nd p. after p. 48.

9. Ibid.

10. *Praeraphaelite Diaries and Letters*, ed. William Michael Rossetti (London, 1900), p. 207.

11. *Ruskin: Rossetti: Preraphaelitism. Papers: 1854 to 1862*, ed. William Michael Rossetti (London, 1899), p. 221.

Chapter Three

1. *Ruskin: Rossetti: Preraphaelitism*, pp. 258–59.

2. *Letters of Alexander Macmillan*, ed. George Macmillan (Glasgow, 1908), pp. 94–95.

3. B. I. Evans, "The Sources of Christina Rossetti's 'Goblin Market,'" *Modern Language Review* 28 (1933), 156.

4. Ibid., pp. 157–65.

5. *Works*, p. 459.

6. Marian Shalkhauser, "The Feminine Christ," *Victorian Newsletter* 10 (Autumn, 1956), 19–20.

7. A. A. DeVitis, "Goblin Market: Fairy Tale and Reality," *Journal of Popular Culture* 1 (1968), 420.

8. Ibid., p. 421.

9. Violet Hunt, *The Wife of Rossetti* (New York, 1932), p. xiii.

10. Lona Mosk Packer, *Christina Rossetti* (Berkeley, 1963), pp. 149–51.

11. Winston Weathers, "Christina Rossetti: The Sisterhood of Self," *Victorian Poetry* 3 (Spring, 1965), 81–89.

12. Ibid., p. 82.

13. Ibid., p. 83.

14. Ibid., p. 89.

15. Wendell S. Johnson, "Some Functions of Poetic Form," *Journal of Aesthetics and Art Criticism* (June, 1955), p. 504.

16. In a letter to the editor, *The New York Times Book Review*, Feb. 2, 1964, p. 28.

Chapter Four

1. *Works*, p. liv.

2. Ibid.

3. *The Family Letters of Christina Georgina Rossetti*, p. 103.

4. *Works*, p. lvi.

5. Ibid., p. lxviii.

6. *Letter and Spirit: Notes on the Commandments* (London [1883]), p. 104.

7. Elizabeth Jennings, *A Choice of Christina Rossetti's Verse* (London, 1970), p. 12.

8. *Works*, p. lxvii.

9. Ibid., pp. lxvii–lxviii.

10. Ibid., p. lxviii.

11. James Kohl, "A Medical Comment on Christina Rossetti," *Notes and Queries* 15 (Nov., 1968), 423–24.

12. *Works*, pp. liv–lv.

13. The speaker in the poems is assumed to be a woman unless the context clearly indicates otherwise.

14. K. E. Janowitz, "The Antipodes of Self: Three Poems by Christina Rossetti," *Victorian Poetry* 11 (Autumn, 1973), 195.

15. Packer, p. 231.

16. Alice Meynell, "Christina Rossetti," *Living Age* 204 (March 2, 1895), 571.

17. For a discussion of the imagery in the poem, see Richard D. Lynde, "A Note on the Imagery in Christina Rossetti's 'A Birthday,' " *Victorian Poetry* 3 (Autumn, 1965), 261–63.

18. Conrad Festa in "Symbol and Meaning in 'A Birthday,' " *English Language Notes* 11 (1973), 50–56, sees the lover in the poem as Christ and the event as Christina's imagined resurrection after death.

19. *The Rossetti-Macmillan Letters*, ed. Lona Mosk Packer (Berkeley, 1963), p. 99.

20. Ellen A. Proctor, *A Brief Memoir of Christina G. Rossetti* (1895; reprint. Folcroft, Pennsylvania, 1969), p. 82.

21. *Works*, p. 489.

Chapter Five

1. Mackenzie Bell, *Christina Rossetti* (London, 1898), p. 225.

2. *Works*, p. 462.

3. Ibid.

4. William Michael wrote that Sonnet 27 fairly accurately forecasts the last days before Christina's own death. See *Works*, p. 463.

5. T. Hall Caine, *Recollections of Dante Gabriel Rossetti* (London, 1882), pp. 247–48.

Chapter Six

1. Anon., "Christina Rossetti's Poems," *Catholic World* 24 (Oct., 1876), 126–27.

2. One of her most joyous poems, "A Birthday," was written on Nov. 18, 1857, but some of the poems written shortly before and after are among her most distressing.

3. Paul Elmer More, "Christina Rossetti," in *Shelburne Essays, Third Series*, 1905. New ed. (Boston, 1921), p. 127.

4. *Works*, p. 472.

5. Quoted by More, p. 125.

6. More, p. 126.

7. Packer, p. 156.

8. *Works*, p. 475.

9. Packer, pp. 175–76.

10. *Time Flies: A Reading Diary* (London, 1897), pp. 121–22.

11. *The Family Letters of Christina Georgina Rossetti*, p. 164.

12. Oliver Elton, *A Survey of English Literature: 1780–1880* (New York, 1920), IV, 29–30.

Chapter Seven

1. Barbara Garlitz, "Christina Rossetti's *Sing-Song* and Nineteenth-Century Children's Poetry," *Publications of the Modern Language Association of America* 70 (1955), 539.

Chapter Eight

1. *Commonplace and Other Short Stories* (London, 1870), p. 140.

2. Ibid., pp. 101–2.

3. Ibid., p. 105.

4. In a letter to Alice Boyd. *Letters of Dante Gabriel Rossetti*, ed. Oswald Doughty and John Robert Wahl (Oxford, 1965), II, 818.

5. For a discussion of the autobiographical aspects of the story see Packer, *Christina Rossetti*, pp. 271–2.

6. *Commonplace*, p. 211.

7. *Letters of Dante Gabriel Rossetti*, II, 586.

8. *Commonplace*, p. 208.

9. Ibid., p. 251.

10. Ibid., p. 253.

11. Ibid., p. 267.

12. *Letters of Dante Gabriel Rossetti*, II, 827.

13. Bell, *Christina Rossetti*, p. 278.

14. *The Family Letters of Christina Georgina Rossetti*, Letter to Dante Gabriel, May 4, 1874, pp. 43–44.

15. *The Rossetti-Macmillan Letters*, p. 101.

16. *Speaking Likenesses* (London, 1874), pp. 17–18.

17. Ibid., p. 28.

18. Ibid.

19. Ibid., pp. 48–49.

20. Ibid., p. 77.

21. Anon., "Not All Roses in the Victorian Nursery," *Times Literary Supplement*, Children's Section (May 29, 1959), p. xi, and Lona Mosk Packer's comment in *Times Literary Supplement* (June 5, 1959), p. 337.

22. "Not All Roses in the Victorian Nursery," p. xi.

23. *Speaking Likenesses*, p. 71.

Chapter Nine

1. *Annus Domini: A Prayer for Each Day of the Year, Founded on a Text of Holy Scripture* (London, 1874), p. iii.

2. *The Family Letters of Christina Georgina Rossetti*, Letter dated July 25, 1879?, pp. 80–81.

3. *Letters of Dante Gabriel Rossetti*, IV, 1676.

4. *Seek and Find: A Double Series of Short Studies of the Benedicite* (London, [1879]), p. 43.

5. Gisela Hönnighausen, "Emblematic Tendencies in the Works of Christina Rossetti," *Victorian Poetry* 10 (Spring, 1972), 2, fn. 1.

6. *Seek and Find*, pp. 197–98.

7. Ibid., p. 37.

8. *Called to be Saints: The Minor Festivals Devotionally Studied* (London [1881]), p. xiii.

9. For a thorough examination of Christina's use of the emblematic mode in her prose and poetry, see Hönninghausen's "Emblematic Tendencies in the Works of Christina Rossetti" and her dissertation, "Christina Rossetti als viktorianische Dichterin" (Bonn, 1969).

10. *Letter and Spirit*, p. 200.

11. *Christina Rossetti*, p. 365.

12. *Times Flies: A Reading Diary* (London, 1885), p. 3.

13. Ibid., p. 5.

14. Ibid., p. 26.

15. *The Face of the Deep: A Devotional Commentary on the Apocalypse* (London, 1892), p. 7.

16. In a letter to Theodore Watts-Dunton, dated Nov. 22 [1886?], British Museum, Ashley MS, p. 23.

17. *The Face of the Deep*, p. 11.

18. *The Family Letters of Christina Georgina Rossetti*, p. 103.

19. *The Face of the Deep*, p. 551.

Selected Bibliography

PRIMARY SOURCES

An annotated list of manuscript holdings is given in Lona Mosk Packer's *Christina Rossetti* (Berkeley: Univ. of California Press, 1963), pp. 435–39.

1. Books by Christina Rossetti

Verses. London: Privately printed by Gaetano Polidori, 1847.
Goblin Market and Other Poems. London: Macmillan, 1862.
The Prince's Progress and Other Poems. London: Macmillan, 1866.
Commonplace and Other Short Stories. London: F. S. Ellis, 1870.
Sing-Song: A Nursery Rhyme Book. London: George Routledge, 1872.
Annus Domini: A Prayer for Each Day of the Year, Founded on a Text of Holy Scripture. London: James Parker, 1874.
Speaking Likenesses. London: Macmillan, 1874.
Goblin Market, The Prince's Progress, and Other Poems. London: Macmillan, 1875.
Seek and Find. London: Society for Promoting Christian Knowledge, 1879.
A Pageant and Other Poems. London: Macmillan, 1881.
Called to be Saints: The Minor Festivals Devotionally Studied. London: Society for Promoting Christian Knowledge, 1881.
Letter and Spirit. London: Society for Promoting Christian Knowledge, 1883.
Time Flies: A Reading Diary. London: Society for Promoting Christian Knowledge, 1885.
Poems. New and Enlarged Edition. London: Macmillan, 1890.
The Face of the Deep: A Devotional Commentary on the Apocalypse. London: Society for Promoting Christian Knowledge, 1892.
Verses. Reprinted from *Called to be Saints, Time Flies*, and *The Face of the Deep*. London: Society for Promoting Christian Knowledge, 1893.
New Poems, Hitherto Unpublished or Uncollected. Ed. William Michael Rossetti. London: Macmillan, 1896.
Maude: A Story for Girls. With an Introduction by William M. Rossetti. London: James Bowden, 1897.

127

The Poetical Works of Christina Georgina Rossetti. Ed. William Michael
Rossetti. London: Macmillan, 1904. Includes a preface, a memoir,
notes, and other useful editorial matter. The arrangement, as well as
other features, presents difficulties.

2. Correspondence

DOUGHTY, OSWALD and JOHN ROBERT WAHL, eds. *Letters of Dante Gabriel
Rossetti.* 4 vols. Oxford: Clarendon Press, 1965–67. The most extensive collection of letters of Dante Gabriel. Includes letters to
Christina, to Mrs. Rossetti (many probably intended for Christina's
reading as well), and to others in which Christina is mentioned.

PACKER, LONA MOSK, ed. *The Rossetti-Macmillan Letters: Some 133
Unpublished Letters Written to Alexander Macmillan, F. S. Ellis, and
Others, by Dante Gabriel, Christina, and William Michael Rossetti,
1861–1889.* Berkeley: Univ. of California Press, 1963. Contains
ninety-six letters written by Christina in the years 1861–1889, more
than half of them to Alexander Macmillan. They reveal her "as the
working poet with a business-like interest in preparing her books for
publication."

ROSSETTI, WILLIAM MICHAEL, ed. *Dante Gabriel Rossetti: His Family
Letters, with a Memoir.* 2 vols. London: Ellis, 1895. Vol. 1 is a
Memoir. Vol. 2 contains letters to William Michael, Mrs. Rossetti, and
Christina, among other family members. Though vol. 2 has been
superseded by *Letters of Dante Gabriel Rossetti,* ed. Doughty and
Wahl, now standard, William Michael's volumes are still useful.

———. *The Family Letters of Christina Georgina Rossetti, with Some Sup-
plementary Letters and Appendices.* London: Brown, Langham,
1908. Also includes extracts from the Diary of William Michael Rossetti, 1871–1895, and the Diary of Mrs. Rossetti kept by Christina,
1881–1886.

———. *Praeraphaelite Diaries and Letters.* London: Hurst and Blackett,
1900. Contains some early letters (1835–54) of Dante Gabriel Rossetti, extracts from the diary of Ford Madox Brown, and "The P. R. B.
Journal" for the period from May, 1849 to May, 1853.

———. *Rossetti Papers, 1862–1870.* London: Sands, 1903. In addition to
fourteen letters by Christina, the volume includes letters by many
hands and extracts from William Michael's diary. Numerous comments on poems by Christina.

———. *Ruskin: Rossetti: Preraphaelitism. Papers 1854 to 1862.* London:
Allen, 1899. Collection of letters mainly concerning John Ruskin and
Dante Gabriel Rossetti in the years 1854–62; includes references to
Christina and her poetry, and a note and letter written by her.

TROXELL, JANET CAMP, ed. *Three Rossettis: Unpublished Letters to and
from Dante Gabriel, Christina, William.* Cambridge: Harvard Univ.
Press, 1937. Chapters 9 and 10 contain thirty-two letters by Christina

and background commentary by Troxell, as well as many pertinent quotations from other letters.

SECONDARY SOURCES

1. Bibliographical

ANDERSON, J. P. "Bibliography" in Mackenzie Bell's *Christina Rossetti*. London: Hurst and Blackett, 1898, pp. 339–53. The first attempt at a complete bibliography of primary and secondary sources.

EHRSAM, THEODORE G., ROBERT H. DEILY, AND ROBERT M. SMITH. "Christina Georgina Rossetti." In *Bibliographies of Twelve Victorian Authors*. New York: Wilson, 1936, pp. 189–99. Still useful bibliography.

FREDEMAN, WILLIAM E. "Christina Rossetti." *The Victorian Poets: A Guide to Research*. Ed. Frederic E. Faverty. Cambridge: Harvard Univ. Press, 1968, pp. 284–93. Valuable critical commentary on a number of major works.

———. *Pre-Raphaelitism: A Bibliocritical Study*. Cambridge: Harvard Univ. Press, 1965. Most extensive and authoritative bibliocritical survey of Pre-Raphaelitism. Indispensable for anyone working with any of the Pre-Raphaelites and those associated with them.

PACKER, LONA MOSK. *Christina Rossetti*. Berkeley: Univ. of California Press, 1963. Includes a convenient working bibliography.

SLACK, ROBERT C., ed. *Bibliographies of Studies in Victorian Literature for the Ten Years 1955–1964*. Urbana: Univ. of Illinois Press, 1967.

TEMPLEMAN, WILLIAM D., ed. *Bibliographies of Studies in Victorian Literature for the Thirteen Years, 1932–1944*. Urbana: Univ. of Illinois Press, 1945.

WEIDEMAN, REBECCA SUE. "A Critical Bibliography of Christina Rossetti." Ph.D. Diss., University of Texas at Austin, 1970. Helpful annotations on most of the published materials. Available from University Microfilms.

WRIGHT, AUSTIN, ed. *Bibliographies of Studies in Victorian Literature for the Ten Years 1945–1954*. Urbana: Univ. of Illinois Press, 1956.

2. Biographical and Critical

BALD, MARJORY A. "Christina Rossetti: 1830–1894." *Women-Writers of the Nineteenth Century*. First published in 1923. New York: Russell & Russell, 1963, pp. 233–84. Christina's renunciation, awareness of the shadow of death, and her religion help explain the "sensitive quality" of her poetry.

BATTISCOMBE, GEORGINA. *Christina Rossetti*. London: Longmans, Green, 1965. Introductory study in the Writers and Their Work series for the British Council and the National Book League. Pre-Raphaelitism and the Oxford Movement seen as the major forces shaping her poetry.

BELL, MACKENZIE. *Christina Rossetti*. London: Hurst and Blackett, 1898. First full-length biographical-critical study; written with the close cooperation of William Michael Rossetti. Bell considered himself not so much a critic as an "exponent" of Christina and her work. Contains some letters and other material not elsewhere available. Remains an essential source of information.

BIRKHEAD, EDITH. *Christina Rossetti and Her Poetry*. London: Harrap, 1930. Christina was uninfluenced by the times or by contemporary writers. She lived in her own private world: "Her lyrics form a spiritual biography."

BOWRA, C. M. "Christina Rossetti." *The Romantic Imagination*. Cambridge: Harvard Univ. Press. 1949. Christina seen as a poet with a dual personality writing Pre-Raphaelite poetry of "imagination and fancy" and poetry of devotion. The basic conflict in her life was between "the woman and the saint."

CARY, ELISABETH L. *The Rossettis: Dante Gabriel and Christina*. New York: Putnam, 1900. "Sincerity and fervour" characterize her secular and religious verse. "Monna Innominata" given special praise as her most subjective work.

CURRAN, STUART. "The Lyric Voice of Christina Rossetti." *Victorian Poetry* 9 (Autumn, 1971), 287–99. An uneven poet, Christina is, nonetheless, "a gifted minor one with a remarkable ease of spontaneous melody and occasional moments of compressed energy suggestive of powers never fully developed."

ELTON, OLIVER. "The Rossettis." *A Survey of English Literature: 1780–1880*. New York: Macmillan, 1920, IV, 1–30. A spontaneous poet, Christina wrote three kinds of verse: fantastic, religious, and impassioned secular.

EVANS, B. I. "The Sources of Christina Rossetti's 'Goblin Market.' " *Modern Language Review* 28 (1933), 156–65. Certain elements in the poem traced to Christina's reading and experiences.

EVANS, IFOR. *English Poetry in the Later Nineteenth Century*. 2nd ed. rev. New York: Barnes & Noble, 1966. An overview of the major and minor poets from 1860–1900, but excluding the work of Tennyson, Browning, and Arnold. Chapter 3 (pp. 87–103) is devoted to Christina Rossetti.

FAIRCHILD, HOXIE NEALE. "Christina Rossetti." *Religious Trends in English Poetry*. Vol. IV: 1830–1880. *Christianity and Romanticism in the Victorian Era*. New York: Columbia Univ. Press, 1957, pp. 302–16. Her work exhibits an "overstrained and unhealthy" piety.

FRASER, ROBERT S., ed. "Essays on the Rossettis," *The Princeton University Library Chronicle* 33 (Spring, 1972), 139–256. Seven essays based on materials in the important Rossetti collection of Janet Camp Troxell acquired by the Princeton University Library.

GARLITZ, BARBARA. "Christina Rossetti's *Sing-Song* and Nineteenth-Century Children's Poetry." *PMLA* 70 (1955), 539–43. At least half of

the poems in *Sing-Song* are related to the moral and sentimental
tradition in nineteenth-century children's verse.

The Germ. London: Stock, 1901; rpt. New York: AMS, 1965. Photo-
facsimile of Elliot Stock's type-facsimile of the original *Germ*. For a
discussion of the various reprints of *The Germ*, see William E.
Fredeman's review of *The Germ: A Pre-Raphaelite Little Magazine*,
ed. Robert Stahr Hosmon, Univ. of Miami Press, 1971, in *Victorian
Poetry* 10 (Spring, 1972), 87–94.

GOSSE, SIR EDMUND. "Christina Rossetti." *Critical Kit-Kats*. London:
Heinemann, 1896. The main part of the essay first appeared in *Century Magazine* 46, n.s. 24 (June, 1893), 211–17. In the lyrics, "her
habitual tone is one of melancholy reverie, the pathos of which is
strangely intensified by her appreciation of beauty and pleasure."
Her best sonnets have the "peculiarity" of being objective.

HÖNNIGHAUSEN, GISELA. "Emblematic Tendencies in the Works of
Christina Rossetti." *Victorian Poetry* 10 (Spring, 1972), 1–15. Significant study of the "emblematic mode of expression" in Christina's
prose and poetry.

HOUGHTON, WALTER E., and G. ROBERT STANGE, eds. *Victorian Poetry and
Poetics*. 2nd ed. Boston: Houghton Mifflin, 1968. Brief introduction
to the poems of Christina Rossetti is excellent in pointing out features
that relate her work to other Victorians and to the modern tradition.

HUEFFER, FORD MADOX. "The Character of Christina Rossetti." *Fortnightly
Review* 95 (March, 1911), 422–29. Praises Christina as a great "master
of words"; considers her modern because much of her poetry is introspective.

HUNT, VIOLET. *The Wife of Rossetti*. New York: Dutton, 1932. Un-
sympathetic treatment of Christina in a book that exploits the sen-
sational.

IRONSIDE, ROBIN. "Introduction." *Poems by Christina Rossetti*. London:
Grey Walls Press, 1953. Perceptive essay on keys to her personality
and poetry.

JANOWITZ, K. E. "The Antipodes of Self: Three Poems by Christina
Rossetti." *Victorian Poetry* 2 (1973), 195–205. Penetrating analysis of
the theme of disillusionment and loss in "Spring," "Restive," and
"Acme."

LYNDE, RICHARD D. "A Note on the Imagery in Christina Rossetti's 'A
Birthday.'" *Victorian Poetry* 3 (1965), 261–63. Study of sources for
the imagery in "A Birthday" that illustrates Christina's "freely as-
sociative method" of composition.

MOORE, VIRGINIA. "Christina Rossetti." *Distinguished Women Writers*.
New York: Dutton, 1934, pp. 43–58. Fear was at the root of
Christina's character.

MORE, PAUL ELMER. "Christina Rossetti." *Shelburne Essays, Third Series*.
1905. New ed. Boston: Houghton Mifflin, 1921, pp. 124–42. Much of
her poetry is like "the continuous lisping of an aeolian harp," but in

some of it "there sounds a strain of wonderful beauty and flawless perfection." The special quality of her verse is attributed to her passiveness and her willingness to express "feminine" attitudes and emotions.

PACKER, LONA MOSK. *Christina Rossetti.* Berkeley: Univ. of California Press, 1963. Most significant biography; but is controversial because of its claim that it was William Bell Scott, not two previously acknowledged suitors, James Collinson and Charles Bagot Cayley, who inspired her love poems and "crucially shaped her life, developed her character, and finally made her into the woman she eventually became."

——. "Symbol and Reality in Christina Rossetti's *Goblin Market.*" *PMLA,* 73 (1958), 375–85. Analysis of the poem on the narrative, allegorical, and psychological levels. The temptation theme is given personal relevance because of Christina's alleged love for William Bell Scott.

PROCTOR, ELLEN A. *A Brief Memoir of Christina G. Rossetti.* London: Society for Promoting Christian Knowledge, 1895. Of interest for Christina's attitudes during the last years of her life and final illness, as revealed during visits by the author and in an exchange of correspondence.

ROBB, NESCA A. "Christina Rossetti." *Four in Exile.* London: Hutchinson, 1948. Central thesis of Christina's poetry seen as a belief that all share in the pain of having lost Eden — the biblical Eden and the Eden that was childhood. Transient joys of life lead but to death, dreaded perhaps, but sought also as the only way to a new Eden.

ROSSETTI, WILLIAM MICHAEL, ed. "Memoir." *The Poetical Works of Christina Georgina Rossetti.* London: Macmillan, 1904. Contains important background information. Includes a list of portraits of Christina.

——. *Some Reminiscences.* 2 vols. London: Brown Langham, 1906. First-hand details of the Rossetti family life. Of special interest are William's accounts of Christina's engagement to Collinson and of her love for Cayley.

SAINTSBURY, GEORGE. *A History of English Prosody.* London: Macmillan, 1910. III, 352–59. Christina has great skill in handling irregular measures. "Goblin Market" is a prosodic masterpiece.

SANDARS, MARY F. *The Life of Christina Rossetti.* London: Hutchinson, 1930. Brings together a considerable amount of information on Christina's life and publications.

SAWTELL, MARGARET. *Christina Rossetti: Her Life and Religion.* London: Mowbray, 1955. Highly sympathetic study of Christina's religious views and poetry; work intended as a corrective to the charge of morbidity in her life and work.

SCOTT, WILLIAM BELL. *Autobiographical Notes . . . and Notices of his Artistic and Poetic Circle of Friends, 1830 to 1882.* Ed. W. Minto. 2

vols. London: Osgood, 1892. Contains only a few references to Christina Rossetti but an important source for information on Scott for those who want to pursue Packer's thesis that Scott was a major influence in Christina's life.

SHARP, WILLIAM. "Some Reminiscences of Christina Rossetti." *The Atlantic Monthly* 75 (June, 1895), 736–49. A eulogy on Christina by one who knew her in her later years.

SHOVE, FREDEGOND. *Christina Rossetti*. London: Cambridge Univ. Press, 1931. Brief appreciation of Christina's life, poetry, and prose. "Christina Rossetti was not only an artist, but was also a great spirit, a woman whose beautiful soul and high moral character matched all her beauty in prayer as in poetry." "Her religion informed and invigorated all her points of view."

STEVENSON, LIONEL. "Christina Rossetti." *The Pre-Raphaelite Poets*. Chapel Hill: Univ. of North Carolina Press, 1972, pp. 78–122. Christina's contribution to English poetry is more extensive than generally acknowledged.

STUART, DOROTHY M. *Christina Rossetti*. London: Macmillan, 1930. Though Christina wrote under Pre-Raphaelite influence, influence has been exaggerated. Her most characteristic poems show slight Pre-Raphaelite influence. These are unadorned lyrics, pure and eloquent.

SWANN, THOMAS BURNETT. *Wonder and Whimsy: The Fantastic World of Christina Rossetti*. Francestown: Marshall Jones, 1960. Christina's claim to uniqueness rests on a select group of poems of fancy that exhibit "wonder" and "whimsy."

THOMAS, ELEANOR W. *Christina Georgina Rossetti*. New York: Columbia Univ. Press, 1931. Special effort to see Christina's work in relation to her own period and to contemporary writers. Christina forsakes the finite in a "Quest for the Infinite."

WALLER, R. D. *The Rossetti Family, 1824–1854*. Manchester: Manchester Univ. Press, 1932. Full and scholarly work on Gabriele Rossetti, with a chapter on the lives of the four Rossetti children up to 1854, the year of Gabriele's death. Invaluable for the early years.

WATTS-DUNTON, THEODORE. "Reminiscences of Christina Rossetti." *The Nineteenth Century* 37 (Feb., 1895), 355–66. As a close friend of Dante Gabriel from 1872–1882, Watts-Dunton knew Christina and regarded her as "the most adored personality among the poets of our time."

WEATHERS, WINSTON. "Christina Rossetti: The Sisterhood of Self." *Victorian Poetry* 3 (1965), 81–89. The "sister" poems seen as studies in which Christina mythicized her divided ego and struggled for "psychological integration." A provocative article that indicates one direction serious criticism of Christina will take in the future.

WINWAR, FRANCES [FRANCES GREBANIER]. *Poor Splendid Wings: The Rossettis and Their Circle*. Boston: Little, Brown, 1933. Sees Christina's love for James Collinson continuing long after the engage-

ment was canceled. Also emphasizes Christina's withdrawal and
resentment when Elizabeth Siddal came into Dante Gabriel's life.
Takes some freedom in recreating characters and events.

WOOLF, VIRGINIA. "I Am Christina Rossetti." *Second Common Reader.*
New York: Harcourt, Brace, 1932, pp. 257–65. Christina was an in-
stinctive poet, and her poetry must speak for her rather than the incidents of her life.

ZATURENSKA, MARYA. *Christina Rossetti: A Portrait with Background.* New
York: Macmillan, 1949. Though influenced by Violet Hunt's *The
Wife of Rossetti*, the full study gives a fairly well balanced picture of
Christina. Gibes, however, do occur here and there.

Index

(The works of Christina Rossetti are listed under her name. Untitled poems are listed under first lines; poems with the same title have first lines in parentheses)